RAIL ATLAS
GREAT BRITAIN
& IRELAND

Compiled by **S.K. Baker**

Haynes

Oxford Publishing Co.

A FOULIS-OPC RAILWAY Book

Fifth Edition
© 1988 S.K. Baker & Haynes Publishing Group
Reprinted 1988

Published by:
Haynes Publishing Group,
Sparkford, Near Yeovil, Somerset, BA22 7JJ

Haynes Publications Inc.
861 Lawrence Drive, Newbury Park, California 91320, USA.

British Library Cataloguing in Publication Data
Baker, S.K. (Stuart K.)
  Rail atlas – Great Britain and Ireland. –
  5th ed.
  1.Great Britain. Railways – Atlases
  I. Title   II. Baker, S.K. (Stuart K.) Rail
  atlas of Britain and Ireland
  912'.1385'0941
  ISBN 0-86093-419-5

517 .

To Helena
love Katherine - Alasdair

PREFACE TO FIRST EDITION

The inspiration for this atlas was two-fold; firstly a feeling of total bewilderment by 'Llans' and 'Abers' on first visiting South Wales four years ago, and secondly a wall railway map drawn by a friend, Martin Bairstow. Since then, at university, there has been steady progress in drawing the rail network throughout Great Britain. The author feels sure that this atlas as it has finally evolved will be useful to all with an interest in railways, whether professional or enthusiast. The emphasis is on the current network since it is felt that this information is not published elsewhere.

Throughout, the main aim has been to show clearly, using expanded sheets where necessary, the railways of this country, including the whole of London Transport and light railways. Passenger lines are distinguished by colour according to operating company and all freight-only lines are depicted in red. The criterion for a British Rail passenger line has been taken as at least one advertised passenger train per day in each direction. On passenger routes, to assist the traveller, single and multiple track sections, with crossing loops on single lines have been shown. Symbols are used to identify both major centres of rail freight, such as collieries and power stations, and railway installations such as locomotive depots and works. Secondary information, for example junction names and tunnels over 100 yards long, with lengths if over one mile has been shown.

The author would like to express his thanks to members of the Oxford University Railway Society and to Nigel Bird, Chris Hammond and Richard Warson in particular for help in compiling and correcting the maps. His cousin, Dr Tony McCann deserves special thanks for removing much of the tedium by computer sorting the index, as do Oxford City Libraries for providing excellent reference facilities.

June 1977

PREFACE TO FIFTH EDITION

This fifth edition of the Rail Atlas of Great Britain and Ireland is fully revised and expanded. The many changes in the rail network are shown along with the numerous proposals for expansion. Nine additional insets clarify the detail within urban areas. New features are the addition of a map showing the extent of electrification systems and the marking of tourist and pleasure railways in blue for extra clarity. The index has been revised and rearranged: junctions and tunnels are indexed for the first time and the passenger and freight sections have been merged for ease of reference.

The author would like to thank the many people who have contacted him to supply material for this new edition. Thanks are also due to his family for their patience and support.

Stuart K. Baker
York
April 1988

CONTENTS

Publisher's Note

Although situations are constantly changing on the railways of Britain every effort has been made by the author to ensure complete accuracy of the maps in the book at the time of going to press.

KEY TO ATLAS

		Surface	Tunnel	Tube
British Rail—Passenger Also Irish and Isle of Man Railways	Multiple Track			
	Single Track			
Municipal Railways (London Underground Ltd — *Line indicated by code,* Tyne & Wear, Greater Manchester, Strathclyde and Blackpool)	Multiple Track			
	Single Track			
Preserved & Minor Passenger Railways *(With name & gauge)*	Multiple Track			
	Single Track			
Freight only lines — *(British Rail & Others)*	No Single/ Multiple Distinction			

Advertised Passenger Station: — Saltburn ●

Crossing Loop at Passenger Station: — Newtown ✕

Crossing Loop on Single Line: — *Kincraig* ✕

Unadvertised/Excursion Station: — Melton* ●

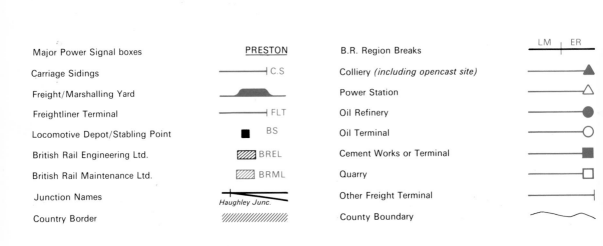

Major Power Signal boxes	PRESTON	B.R. Region Breaks	LM | ER
Carriage Sidings	C.S	Colliery *(including opencast site)*	▲
Freight/Marshalling Yard		Power Station	△
Freightliner Terminal	FLT	Oil Refinery	●
Locomotive Depot/Stabling Point	■ BS	Oil Terminal	○
British Rail Engineering Ltd.	BREL	Cement Works or Terminal	■
British Rail Maintenance Ltd.	BRML	Quarry	□
Junction Names	*Haughley Junc.*	Other Freight Terminal	
Country Border		County Boundary	

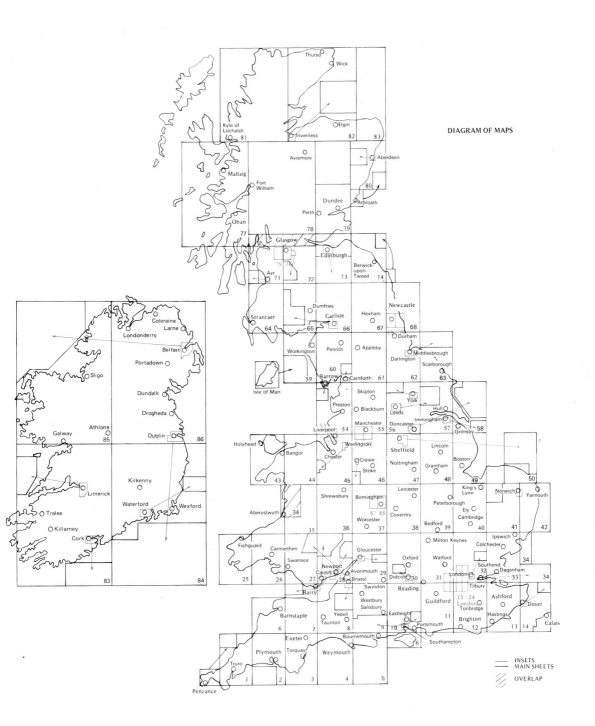

DIAGRAM OF MAPS

INSETS
MAIN SHEETS
OVERLAP

V

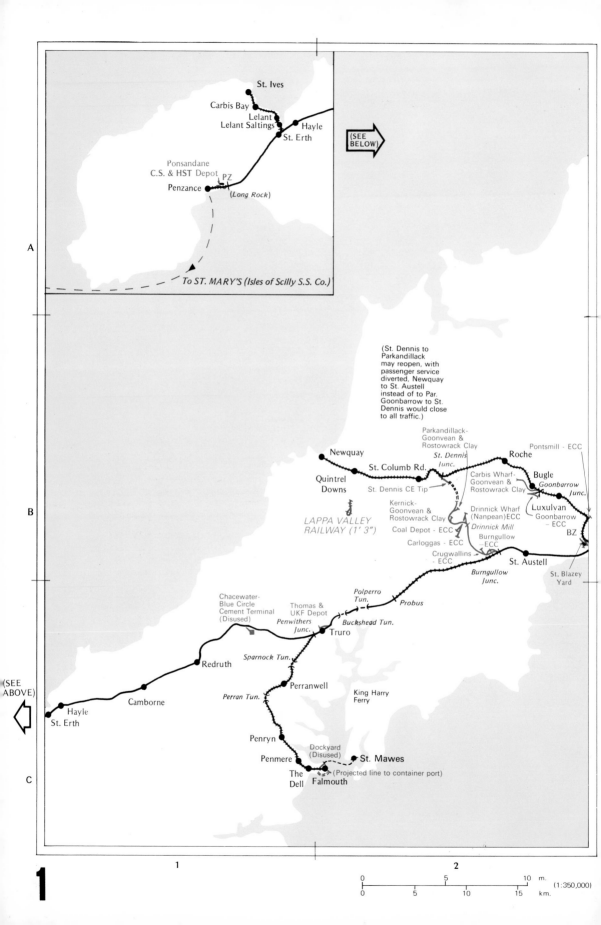

St. Ives

Carbis Bay

Lelant
Lelant Saltings

Hayle

St. Erth

(SEE BELOW)

Ponsandane
C.S. & HST Depot   PZ

Penzance   *(Long Rock)*

To ST. MARY'S (Isles of Scilly S.S. Co.)

A

(St. Dennis to Parkandillack may reopen, with passenger service diverted, Newquay to St. Austell instead of to Par. Goonbarrow to St. Dennis would close to all traffic.)

Parkandillack-
Goonvean &
Rostowrack Clay

*St. Dennis
Junc.*

Pontsmill - ECC

Newquay

St. Columb Rd.

Roche

Quintrel
Downs

St. Dennis CE Tip

Carbis Wharf-
Goonvean &
Rostowrack Clay

Bugle

Goonbarrow

B

*LAPPA VALLEY
RAILWAY (1' 3")*

Kernick-
Goonvean &
Rostowrack Clay

Coal Depot - ECC

Drinnick Wharf
(Nanpean) ECC

Drinnick Mill

Goonbarrow
Junc.

Luxulvan

Goonbarrow
- ECC

BZ

Carloggas - ECC

Burngullow
—ECC

Crugwallins
- ECC

St. Austell

*Burngullow
Junc.*

St. Blazey
Yard

Chacewater-
Blue Circle
Cement Terminal
(Disused)

Thomas &
UKF Depot

*Penwithers
Junc.*

*Polperro
Tun.*

Probus

Buckshead Tun.

Truro

Sparnock Tun.

Redruth

Perranwell

King Harry
Ferry

Perran Tun.

Camborne

Hayle
St. Erth

(SEE
ABOVE)

Penryn

Penmere

Dockyard
(Disused)   St. Mawes

The
Dell   Falmouth   (Projected line to container port)

C

1   2

0   5   10   m.

(1:350,000)

0   5   10   15   km.

1

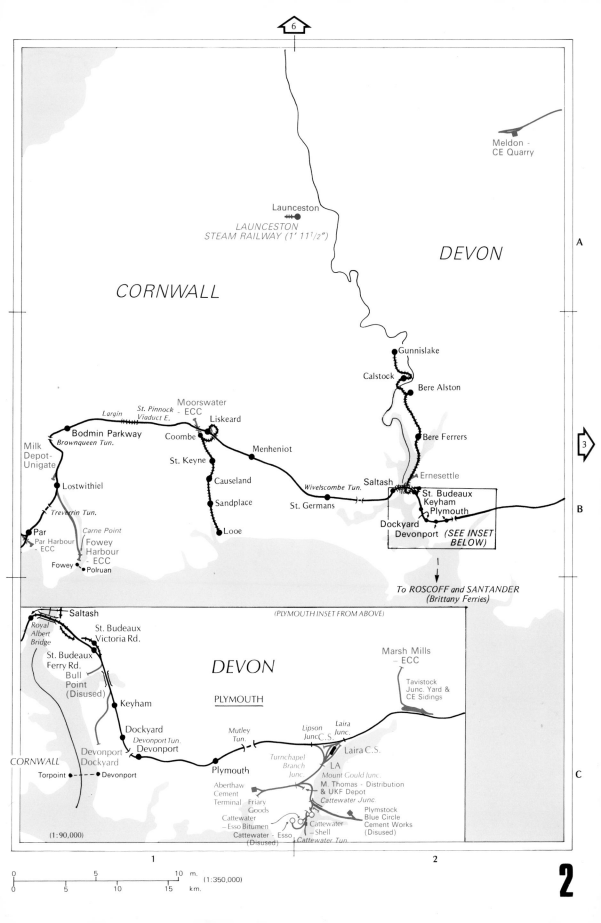

DEVON

Meldon -
CE Quarry

CORNWALL

Launceston

*LAUNCESTON
STEAM RAILWAY (1' 11½")*

A

Gunnislake

Calstock

Bere Alston

Largin   *St. Pinnock
Viaduct E.*   Moorswater
- ECC

Bodmin Parkway   Liskeard

Brownqueen Tun.   Coombe

Milk
Depot-
Unigate   St. Keyne

Lostwithiel   Menheniot

Bere Ferrers

3

Treverrin Tun.   Causeland

Wivelscombe Tun.   Saltash

Ernesettle

St. Budeaux
Keyham
Plymouth

Sandplace   St. Germans

Par
Par Harbour
- ECC   *Carne Point*
Fowey
Harbour
- ECC   Looe

Dockyard
Devonport

*(SEE INSET
BELOW)*

B

Fowey
Polruan

To ROSCOFF and SANTANDER
(Brittany Ferries)

Saltash   *(PLYMOUTH INSET FROM ABOVE)*

*Royal
Albert
Bridge*   St. Budeaux
Victoria Rd.

DEVON

Marsh Mills
- ECC

St. Budeaux
Ferry Rd.
Bull
Point
(Disused)   Keyham

PLYMOUTH

Tavistock
Junc. Yard &
CE Sidings

Dockyard
Devonport Tun.
Devonport

*Mutley
Tun.*   *Lipson
Junc.*C.S.   *Laira
Junc.*

Laira C.S.

CORNWALL   Devonport
Dockyard   LA
Mount Gould Junc.

M. Thomas - Distribution
& UKF Depot
Cattewater Junc.

C

Torpoint   Devonport   Plymouth   *Turnchapel
Branch
Junc.*

Aberthaw
Cement
Terminal   Friary
Goods   Plymstock
Blue Circle
Cement Works
(Disused)

Cattewater
- Esso Bitumen   Cattewater
- Shell

(1:90,000)   Cattewater - Esso
(Disused)   *Cattewater Tun.*

1   2

0   5   10 m.
0   5   10   15 km.   (1:350,000)

2

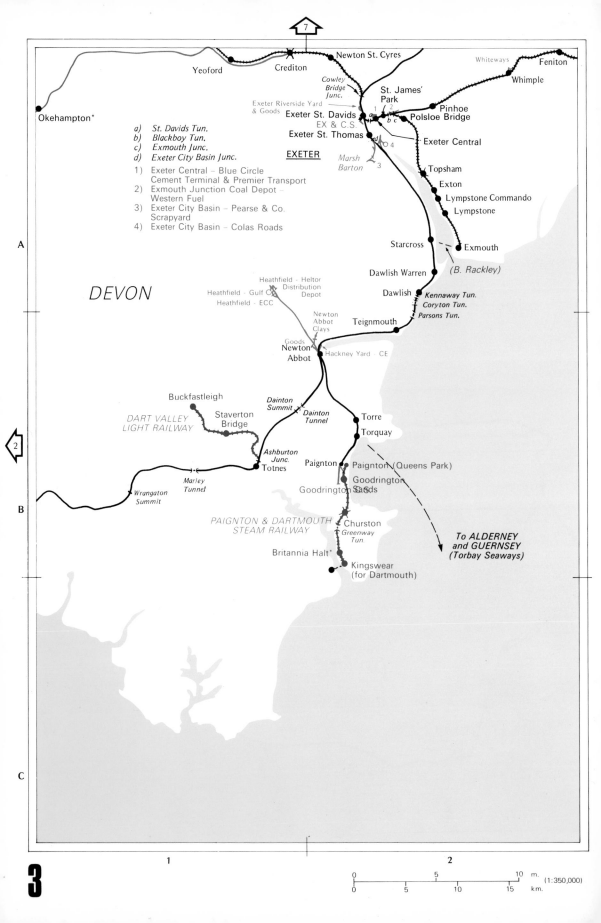

DEVON

Okehampton*

Yeoford

Crediton

Cowley Bridge Junc.

Newton St. Cyres

Whiteways

Feniton

Whimple

Pinhoe

St. James' Park

Exeter Riverside Yard & Goods

Exeter St. Davids

EX & C.S.

Polsloe Bridge

Exeter St. Thomas

Exeter Central

EXETER

a) St. Davids Tun.
b) Blackboy Tun.
c) Exmouth Junc.
d) Exeter City Basin Junc.

1) Exeter Central – Blue Circle Cement Terminal & Premier Transport
2) Exmouth Junction Coal Depot – Western Fuel
3) Exeter City Basin – Pearse & Co. Scrapyard
4) Exeter City Basin – Colas Roads

Marsh Barton

Topsham

Exton

Lympstone Commando

Lympstone

Starcross

Exmouth

(B. Rackley)

Dawlish Warren

Dawlish

Kennaway Tun.
Coryton Tun.
Parsons Tun.

Heathfield – Heltor Distribution Depot
Heathfield – Gulf
Heathfield – ECC

Newton Abbot Clays

Teignmouth

Goods

Newton Abbot

Hackney Yard – CE

Buckfastleigh

DART VALLEY LIGHT RAILWAY

Staverton Bridge

Dainton Summit

Dainton Tunnel

Torre

Torquay

Ashburton Junc.

Totnes

Paignton

Paignton (Queens Park)

Goodrington

Goodrington Sands

Marley Tunnel

Wrangaton Summit

PAIGNTON & DARTMOUTH STEAM RAILWAY

Churston

Greenway Tun.

To ALDERNEY and GUERNSEY (Torbay Seaways)

Britannia Halt*

Kingswear (for Dartmouth)

A

2

B

C

1

2

0   5   10   m.
0   5   10   15   km.

(1:350,000)

3

DEVON

SEATON
TRAMWAY
(2' 9")
Cownhayne

Colyton
Cownhayne
Tye Lane
Colyford
Axmouth
Swan's Nest
Riverside
Seaton   Depot

Axminster

DORSET

Maiden
Newton

8

A

5

B

C

2

4

0   5   10   m.
0   5   10   15   km.
        (1:350,000)

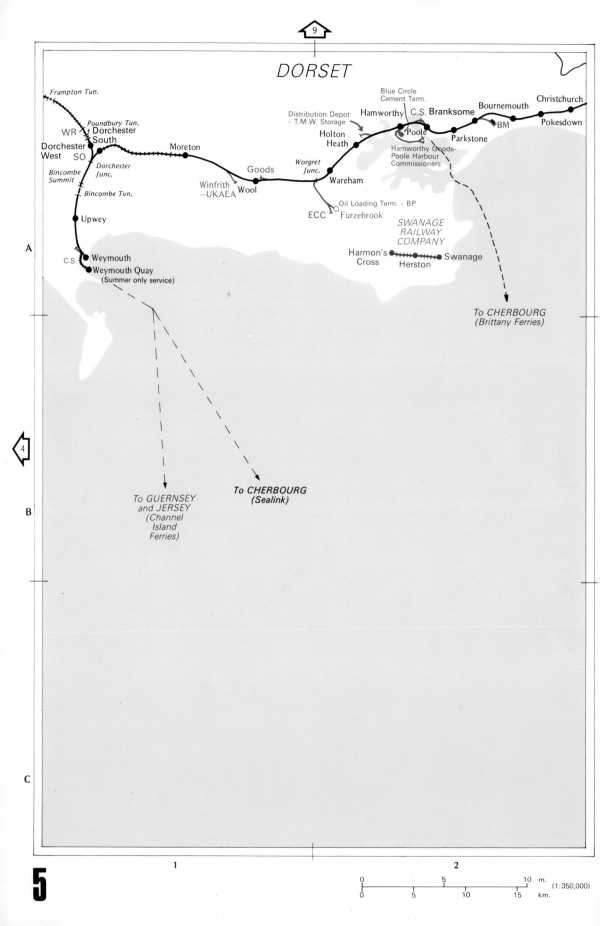

DORSET

Frampton Tun.

Poundbury Tun.

WR Dorchester South

Dorchester West

SO

Bincombe Summit

Dorchester Junc.

Bincombe Tun.

Moreton

Goods

Winfrith —UKAEA

Wool

Worgret Junc.

Wareham

ECC Oil Loading Term. - BP Furzebrook

Upwey

C.S. Weymouth

Weymouth Quay (Summer only service)

Distribution Depot – T.M.W. Storage

Holton Heath

Blue Circle Cement Term.

Hamworthy C.S. Branksome

Poole

Hamworthy Goods- Poole Harbour Commissioners

Parkstone

Bournemouth BM

Christchurch Pokesdown

SWANAGE RAILWAY COMPANY

Harmon's Cross Swanage Herston

To CHERBOURG (Brittany Ferries)

To GUERNSEY and JERSEY (Channel Island Ferries)

To CHERBOURG (Sealink)

9

4

A

B

C

1

2

0   5   10 m.   (1:350,000)

0   5   10   15 km.

5

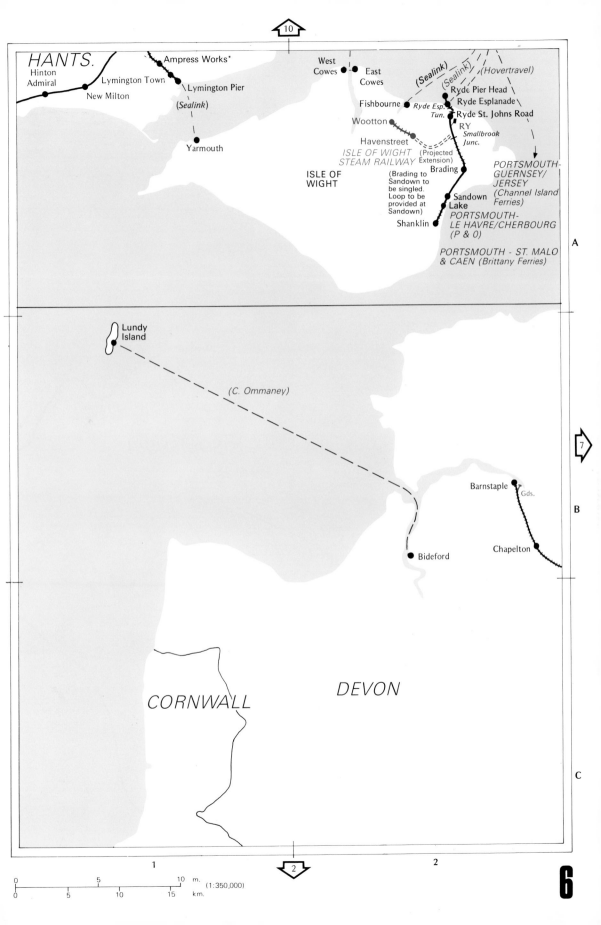

HANTS.

Hinton
Admiral
New Milton
Lymington Town
Ampress Works*
Lymington Pier
(Sealink)
Yarmouth

West
Cowes
East
Cowes
(Sealink)
Fishbourne
Wootton
Havenstreet
ISLE OF WIGHT
STEAM RAILWAY
ISLE OF
WIGHT

(Brading to
Sandown to
be singled.
Loop to be
provided at
Sandown)

Ryde Esp.
Tun.
(Sealink)
(Hovertravel)
Ryde Pier Head
Ryde Esplanade
Ryde St. Johns Road
RY
Smallbrook
Junc.
(Projected
Extension)
Brading
Sandown
Lake
Shanklin

PORTSMOUTH-
GUERNSEY/
JERSEY
(Channel Island
Ferries)

PORTSMOUTH-
LE HAVRE/CHERBOURG
(P & O)

PORTSMOUTH - ST. MALO
& CAEN (Brittany Ferries)

A

Lundy
Island

(C. Ommaney)

Barnstaple
Gds.

Bideford

Chapelton

B

DEVON

CORNWALL

C

1   m.   2
(1:350,000)
km.

0   5   10
0   5   10   15

6

7

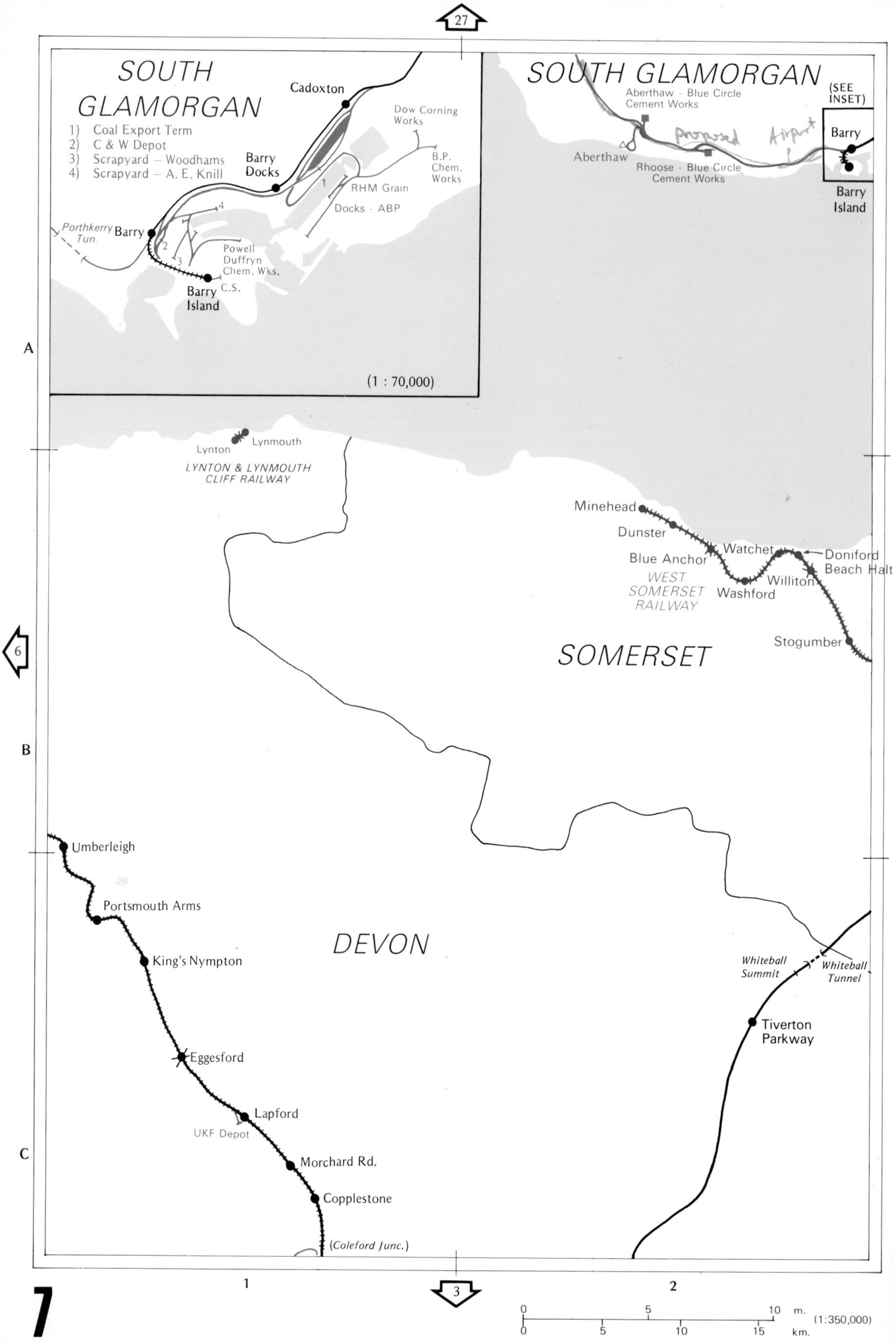

27

SOUTH GLAMORGAN

1) Coal Export Term
2) C & W Depot
3) Scrapyard – Woodhams
4) Scrapyard – A. E. Knill

Cadoxton

Dow Corning Works

Barry Docks

B.P. Chem. Works

RHM Grain

Docks - ABP

Porthkerry Tun.

Barry

Powell Duffryn Chem. Wks.

Barry Island

C.S.

(1 : 70,000)

SOUTH GLAMORGAN

Aberthaw - Blue Circle Cement Works

(SEE INSET)

Aberthaw

Proposed   Airport

Rhoose - Blue Circle Cement Works

Barry

Barry Island

A

Lynton   Lynmouth

LYNTON & LYNMOUTH CLIFF RAILWAY

Minehead

Dunster

Watchet

Blue Anchor

Doniford Beach Halt

Williton

Washford

WEST SOMERSET RAILWAY

Stogumber

SOMERSET

6

B

Umberleigh

Portsmouth Arms

King's Nympton

DEVON

Whiteball Summit

Whiteball Tunnel

Tiverton Parkway

Eggesford

Lapford

UKF Depot

Morchard Rd.

C

Copplestone

(Coleford Junc.)

7

1   3   2

0   5   10 m.   (1:350,000)
0   5   10   15 km.

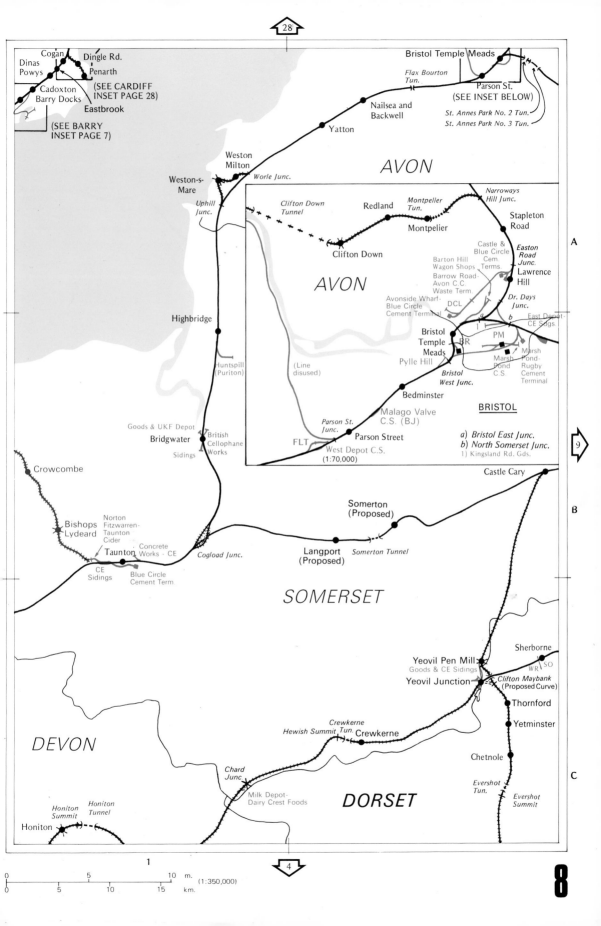

Cogan
Dingle Rd.
Dinas Powys
Penarth
Cadoxton
Barry Docks
Eastbrook
(SEE CARDIFF INSET PAGE 28)
(SEE BARRY INSET PAGE 7)

Bristol Temple Meads
Flax Bourton Tun.
Parson St.
(SEE INSET BELOW)
St. Annes Park No. 2 Tun.
St. Annes Park No. 3 Tun.

Nailsea and Backwell

Yatton

Weston Milton

AVON

Weston-s-Mare
Worle Junc.

Uphill Junc.

AVON (inset)

Clifton Down Tunnel

Redland
Montpelier Tun.
Narroways Hill Junc.
Montpelier
Stapleton Road

Clifton Down

Castle & Blue Circle Cem. Terms.
Easton Road Junc.
Barton Hill Wagon Shops
Lawrence Hill
Barrow Road-Avon C.C. Waste Term.
Dr. Days Junc.
Avonside Wharf-Blue Circle Cement Terminal
DCL
East Depot-CE Sdgs.
(Line disused)
Bristol Temple Meads
BR
PM
Marsh Pond-Rugby Cement Terminal
Pylle Hill
Marsh Pond C.S.

AVON

Highbridge

Huntspill (Puriton)

Bristol West Junc.

Bedminster

BRISTOL

Malago Valve C.S. (BJ)

Parson St. Junc.

Parson Street

a) Bristol East Junc.
b) North Somerset Junc.
1) Kingsland Rd. Gds.

FLT

West Depot C.S.
(1:70,000)

Goods & UKF Depot
Bridgwater
British Cellophane Works
Sidings

Crowcombe

Castle Cary

Somerton (Proposed)

Bishops Lydeard
Norton Fitzwarren-Taunton Cider
Taunton
Concrete Works - CE
Cogload Junc.
Langport (Proposed)
Somerton Tunnel
CE Sidings
Blue Circle Cement Term.

SOMERSET

Sherborne
WR SO
Yeovil Pen Mill
Goods & CE Sidings
Clifton Maybank (Proposed Curve)
Yeovil Junction
Thornford
Yetminster

DEVON

Chard Junc.
Crewkerne
Hewish Summit Tun.
Milk Depot-Dairy Crest Foods
Chetnole

DORSET

Evershot Tun.
Evershot Summit

Honiton Summit
Honiton Tunnel
Honiton

1

0   5   10 m.
0   5   10   15 km.
(1:350,000)

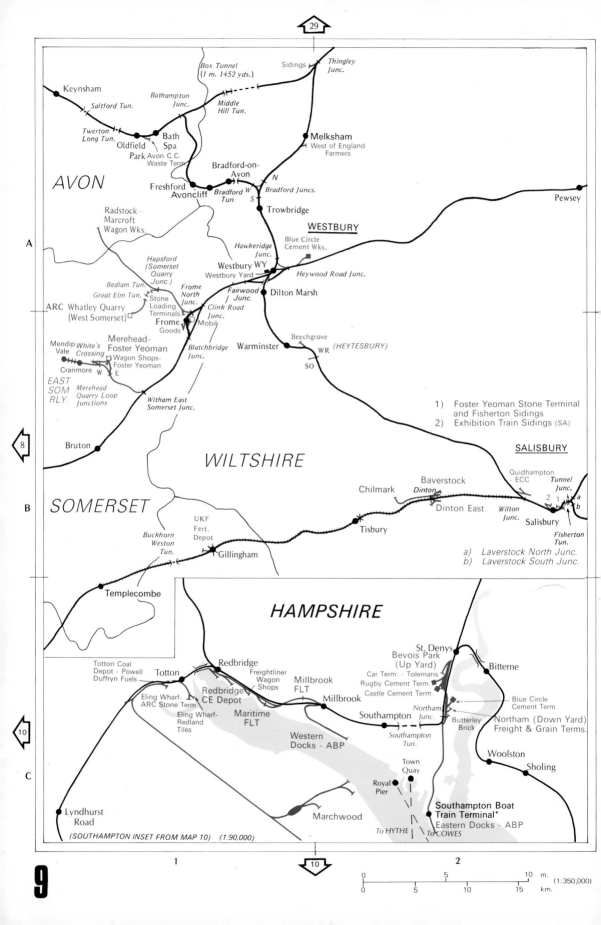

Keynsham

Saltford Tun.

*Box Tunnel
(1 m. 1452 yds.)*

Sidings

*Thingley
Junc.*

*Bathampton
Junc.*

*Middle
Hill Tun.*

*Twerton
Long Tun.*

Oldfield
Park

Bath
Spa

Avon C.C.
Waste Term.

Bradford-on-
Avon

Melksham

West of England
Farmers

AVON

Freshford

Avoncliff

*Bradford
Tun.*

*Bradford
Junc.*

W

N

S

Bradford Juncs.

Trowbridge

Pewsey

Radstock—
Marcroft
Wagon Wks.

WESTBURY

*Hawkeridge
Junc.*

Blue Circle
Cement Wks.

*Hapsford
(Somerset
Quarry
Junc.)*

Westbury WY

Westbury Yard

Heywood Road Junc.

A

Bedlam Tun.

Great Elm Tun.

*Frome
North
Junc.*

*Fairwood
Junc.*

Dilton Marsh

ARC Whatley Quarry
(West Somerset)

Stone
Loading
Terminals

*Clink Road
Junc.*

Mobil

Frome
Goods

Mendip
Vale

*White's
Crossing*

Merehead-
Foster Yeoman

Wagon Shops-
Foster Yeoman

Warminster

Beechgrove

WR (HEYTESBURY)

SO

Cranmore

W

E

*Blatchbridge
Junc.*

*EAST
SOM
RLY.*

*Merehead
Quarry Loop
Junctions*

*Witham East
Somerset Junc.*

1) Foster Yeoman Stone Terminal
    and Fisherton Sidings
2) Exhibition Train Sidings (SA)

SALISBURY

Baverstock

Quidhampton
ECC

*Tunnel
Junc.*

Chilmark

Dinton

2 1

a

b

WILTSHIRE

B

SOMERSET

Dinton East

*Wilton
Junc.*

Salisbury

Bruton

Tisbury

a) Laverstock North Junc.
b) Laverstock South Junc.

*Fisherton
Tun.*

UKF
Fert.
Depot

*Buckhorn
Weston
Tun.*

Gillingham

Templecombe

HAMPSHIRE

St. Denys

Bevois Park
(Up Yard)

Bitterne

Totton Coal
Depot - Powell
Duffryn Fuels

Totton

Redbridge

*Freightliner
Wagon
Shops*

Millbrook
FLT

Car Term. - Tolemans
Rugby Cement Term.
Castle Cement Term.

Eling Wharf-
ARC Stone Term

Redbridge
CE Depot

Millbrook

Blue Circle
Cement Term.

Eling Wharf-
Redland
Tiles

Maritime
FLT

Southampton

*Northam
Junc.*

Northam (Down Yard)
Freight & Grain Terms.

Butterley
Brick

Western
Docks - ABP

*Southampton
Tun.*

Woolston

C

Sholing

Town
Quay

Royal
Pier

Lyndhurst
Road

Marchwood

Southampton Boat
Train Terminal*

Eastern Docks - ABP

To HYTHE

To COWES

(SOUTHAMPTON INSET FROM MAP 10) (1:90,000)

A

B

8

10

0 ——————— 5 ——————— 10 m.   (1:350,000)

0 ———— 5 ———— 10 ———— 15 km.

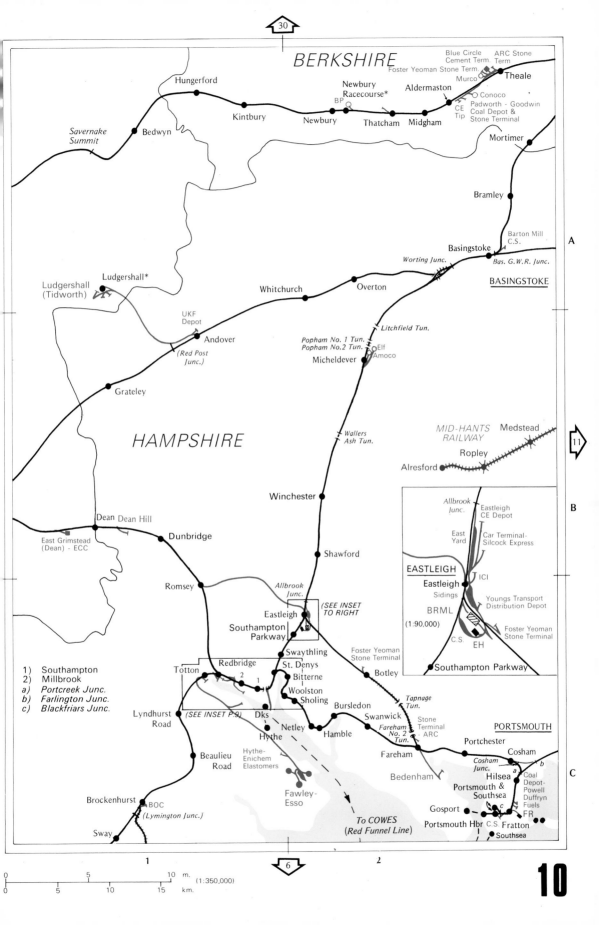

BERKSHIRE

Blue Circle
Cement Term.
ARC Stone
Term.
Foster Yeoman Stone Term.
Theale
Murco
Hungerford
Newbury
Racecourse*
Aldermaston
BP
Conoco
Padworth - Goodwin
Coal Depot &
Stone Terminal
Kintbury
Newbury
Thatcham
Midgham
CE
Tip
Bedwyn
Mortimer
Savernake
Summit
Bramley

Barton Mill
C.S.
Basingstoke
A
Worting Junc.
Bas. G.W.R. Junc.
BASINGSTOKE
Ludgershall*
Whitchurch
Overton
Ludgershall
(Tidworth)
UKF
Depot
Litchfield Tun.
Andover
Popham No. 1 Tun.
Popham No. 2 Tun.
Elf
(Red Post
Junc.)
Micheldever
Amoco
Grateley

HAMPSHIRE
Wallers
Ash Tun.
MID-HANTS
RAILWAY
Medstead

Ropley

Winchester
Alresford

B

Dean Dean Hill
Allbrook
Junc.
Eastleigh
CE Depot
East
Yard
Car Terminal-
Silcock Express
East Grimstead
(Dean) - ECC
Dunbridge
Shawford
EASTLEIGH
ICI
Eastleigh
Romsey
Allbrook
Junc.
Sidings
Youngs Transport
Distribution Depot
Eastleigh
BRML
Southampton
Parkway
(SEE INSET
TO RIGHT)
(1:90,000)
C.S.
Foster Yeoman
Stone Terminal
EH
Swaythling
Foster Yeoman
Stone Terminal
Southampton Parkway

1) Southampton
2) Millbrook
a) Portcreek Junc.
b) Farlington Junc.
c) Blackfriars Junc.

Redbridge
St. Denys
Botley
Totton
2
1
Bitterne
Woolston
Sholing
Bursledon
Tapnage
Tun.
PORTSMOUTH
Lyndhurst
Road
(SEE INSET P.9)
Dks
Swanwick
Fareham
No. 2
Tun.
Stone
Terminal
ARC
Portchester
Cosham
Netley
Hamble
Cosham
Junc.
b
Beaulieu
Road
Hythe-
Enichem
Elastomers
Hythe
Fareham
Bedenham
a
Hilsea
Coal
Depot-
Powell
Duffryn
Fuels
Portsmouth &
Southsea
Brockenhurst
BOC
(Lymington Junc.)
Fawley-
Esso
To COWES
(Red Funnel Line)
Gosport
c
Portsmouth Hbr
C.S. Fratton
FR
Sway
Southsea

1
5
10 m.
(1:350,000)
5
10
15 km.

6

2

30

11

10

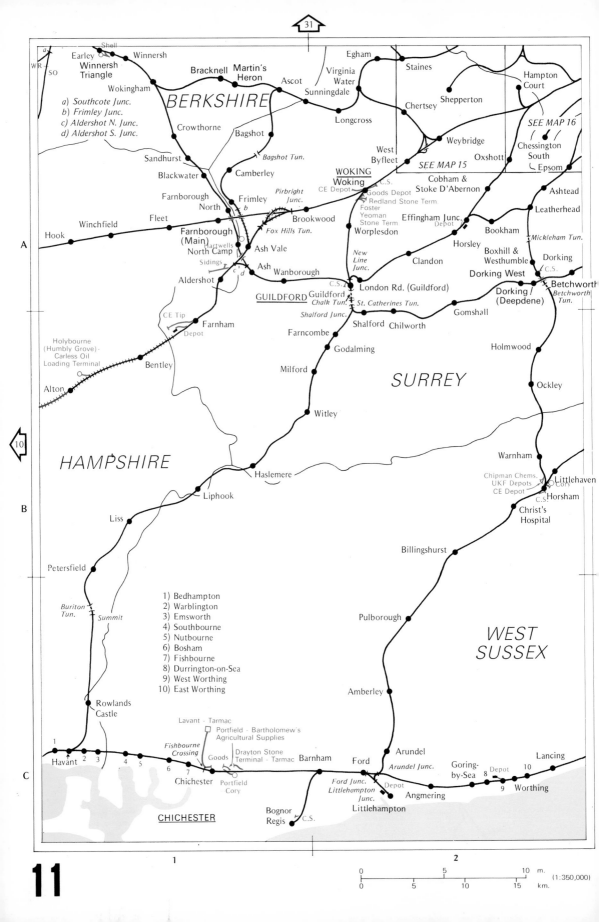

a) Southcote Junc.
b) Frimley Junc.
c) Aldershot N. Junc.
d) Aldershot S. Junc.

BERKSHIRE

Shell
Earley
Winnersh
Winnersh Triangle
Winnersh
Wokingham
Bracknell
Martin's Heron
Ascot
Sunningdale
Crowthorne
Bagshot
Bagshot Tun.
Sandhurst
Blackwater
Camberley
Pirbright Junc.
Farnborough North
Fleet
Frimley
b
Brookwood
Fox Hills Tun.
Winchfield
Farnborough (Main)
Hartwells
North Camp
Sidings
c d
Ash Vale
Hook
Aldershot
Ash
Wanborough
CE Tip
Farnham
Depot
GUILDFORD
Guildford
Chalk Tun.
St. Catherines Tun.
Shalford Junc.
Farncombe
Godalming
Milford
Holybourne (Humbly Grove) - Carless Oil Loading Terminal
Bentley
Alton
Witley

Egham
Staines
Virginia Water
Shepperton
Hampton Court
Chertsey
Longcross
Weybridge
SEE MAP 16
Chessington South
Epsom
West Byfleet
Oxshott
SEE MAP 15
WOKING
Woking
C.S.
CE Depot
Goods Depot
Redland Stone Term.
Foster Yeoman Stone Term.
Cobham & Stoke D'Abernon
Ashtead
Leatherhead
Effingham Junc.
Depot
Worplesdon
Bookham
Mickleham Tun.
Horsley
Boxhill & Westhumble
Dorking
New Line Junc.
Clandon
Dorking West
C.S.
C.S.
London Rd. (Guildford)
Dorking (Deepdene)
Betchworth
Betchworth Tun.
Shalford
Chilworth
Gomshall
Holmwood
Ockley

SURREY

Haslemere
Liphook
HAMPSHIRE
Liss
Petersfield
Buriton Tun.
Summit
Warnham
Chipman Chems.
UKF Depots
CE Depot
Littlehaven
Cory
C.S. Horsham
Christ's Hospital
Billingshurst
Pulborough

WEST SUSSEX

1) Bedhampton
2) Warblington
3) Emsworth
4) Southbourne
5) Nutbourne
6) Bosham
7) Fishbourne
8) Durrington-on-Sea
9) West Worthing
10) East Worthing

Rowlands Castle
Amberley
Lavant - Tarmac
Portfield - Bartholomew's Agricultural Supplies
Fishbourne Crossing
Goods
Drayton Stone Terminal - Tarmac
Barnham
Ford
Arundel
Lancing
1
Havant
2
3
4
5
6
7
Chichester
Portfield Cory
Arundel Junc.
Depot
Ford Junc.
Littlehampton Junc.
Angmering
Goring-by-Sea
Depot
8
9
10
Worthing
CHICHESTER
Bognor Regis
C.S.
Littlehampton

A

10

B

C

WR
SO
a

1
2

0   5   10 m.
0   5   10   15 km.

(1:350,000)

11

Wimbledon

West Croydon

Bromley N.
St. Mary Cray
Farningham Rd.
Longfield
Sole Street
Strood Tun. (1 m. 569 yds.)

Bromley South
Bickley
Petts Wood
Hayes
ON
Orpington
Swanley
Eynsford Tun.
Meopham
Cuxton-Lowfield Distribution
Cuxton
Halling — Rugby Cem. Wks.

Addiscombe
East Croydon
Chelsfield
Eynsford
Halling

See Map 17
GREATER LONDON
Knockholt
Shoreham
Snodland
New Hythe

Sutton
Purley
Riddlesdown
Upper Warlingham
See Map 18
Dunton Green
Otford
Otford Junc.
Kemsing
Brookgate - Reed Paper
Aylesford
West Malling

Banstead
Reedham
Woldingham
Redland Stone Terminal
Bat & Ball
C.S.
Sevenoaks
C.S.
Borough Green & Wrotham
East Malling

Epsom Downs
Coulsdon South
Caterham
Kingswood Tun.
Polhill Tun. (1 m. 851 yds.)
Chelsfield Tun.

8
7
Tadworth
Oxted Tun. (1m 501yds)
OXTED
KENT
Wateringbury

ostham Old Tun. (1 m. 71 yds.)
Merstham
Quarry Tun. (1 m. 353 yds.)
Limpsfield Tun.
Oxted
Sevenoaks Tun. (1 m. 1693 yds.)
Yalding

Redhill C.S.
Holmethorpe — British Ind. Sand.
Redhill Tun.
Hurst Green Junc.
Hurst Green
Hildenborough
C.S.
East Peckham CE Tip
Beltring

Reigate
Hydleman
Nutfield
Godstone
Edenbridge Tun.
Edenbridge
Penshurst
Tonbridge
Transfesa Term.

Earlswood
Bletchingley Tun.
CE Tip
Leigh
West Yard
C.S.
Paddock Wood
Mack & Edwards

Brett Marine Stone Terminal
Salfords
Edenbridge Town
Hever
Mark Beech Tun.
Somerhill Tun.

A

Horley
Gatwick Airport
C.S.
Lingfield
Cowden
Cory Wells Tun.
High Brooms

'Peoplemovers'
RMC Sand Terminal
Foster Yeoman Stone Terminal
Dor to Dor
Crawley New Yard
Dormans
Ashurst
Tunbridge Wells
Grove Hill Tun.

Ifield
THREE BRIDGES
Three Bridges
East Grinstead
Eridge
Strawberry Hill Tun.
Frant

Crawley
Three Bridges CE Depot
(Proposed Extension)
Sharpthorne Tun.
Kingscote
(Hever to Uckfield to be singled, with loops at Ashurst and Crowborough)
Wadhurst
Wadhurst Tun.

Faygate
Balcombe Tun.
West Hoathly
BLUEBELL RAILWAY

Balcombe
Sidings
Ardingly
ARC Stone Terminal
Horsted Keynes
Crowborough
Crowborough Tun.
Stonegate
Etchingham

B

Copyhold Junc.
Freshfield Halt
Haywards Heath
Sheffield Park
Buxted
Mountfield — British Gypsum

Burgess Hill
Wivelsfield
Keymer Junc.
Haywards Heath Tun.
Uckfield

Plumpton
EAST SUSSEX
1) Smitham
2) Woodmansterne
3) Chipstead
4) Whyteleafe South
5) Kenley
6) Whyteleafe
7) Kingswood
8) Tattenham Corner
9) Southwick
10) Fishersgate
11) Portslade
12) Aldrington
a) Cliftonville Tunnel
b) Hove Tunnel
c) Stoats Nest Junc.

Hassocks
Cooksbridge
Clayton Tun. (1 m. 499 yds.)
Lewes Tun.
Collington

Patcham Tun.
Falmer Tun.
Kingston Tun.
Lewes
Normans Bay
Cooden Beach

C.S. & Coal Depot-Powell Duffryn
Preston Park
C.S.
Falmer
Southerham Junc.
Glynde
Berwick
Pevensey Bay

9 10 11 12 a
B1
Moulsecoomb
London Rd. (Brighton)
Southease
Willingdon Junc.
Polegate
Pevensey & Westham

Hove b
Brighton
Marina
Aquarium
Play Centre
Aggregate Loading Term. - RMC
Newhaven Town
Newhaven Harbour
Bishopstone
Hampden Park
C.S.

Shoreham -by-Sea
VOLK'S ELECTRIC RLY. (2' 8½")
Newhaven Marine
To DIEPPE (Sealink)
Southern Port Services
Seaford
Eastbourne

C

13

0   5   10 m.
(1:350,000)
0   5   10   15 km.

1
2

12

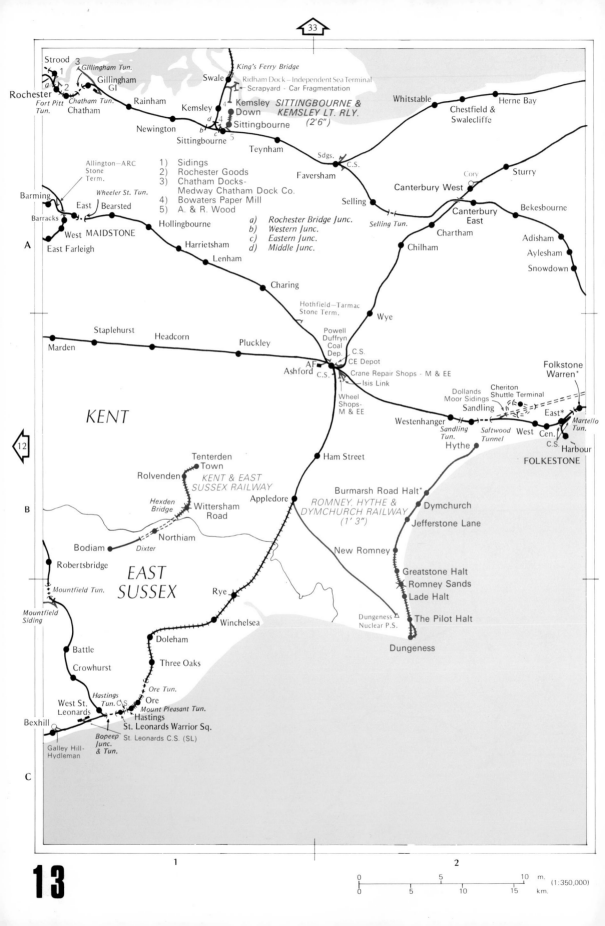

Strood
Gillingham Tun.
Rochester
Gillingham GI
Fort Pitt Tun.
Chatham Tun.
Chatham
Rainham
Newington
Kemsley Down
Sittingbourne
Sittingbourne
Teynham

Swale
King's Ferry Bridge
Ridham Dock – Independent Sea Terminal
Scrapyard - Car Fragmentation
SITTINGBOURNE &
KEMSLEY LT. RLY.
(2'6")

Whitstable
Herne Bay
Chestfield & Swalecliffe

Sdgs.
C.S.
Faversham
Selling
Canterbury West
Cory
Sturry

1) Sidings
2) Rochester Goods
3) Chatham Docks-
   Medway Chatham Dock Co.
4) Bowaters Paper Mill
5) A. & R. Wood

a) *Rochester Bridge Junc.*
b) *Western Junc.*
c) *Eastern Junc.*
d) *Middle Junc.*

Allington–ARC
Stone Term.
Barming
Wheeler St. Tun.
East   Bearsted
Barracks
West   MAIDSTONE
East Farleigh
Hollingbourne
Harrietsham
Lenham
Charing

Canterbury East
Bekesbourne
Chartham
Adisham
Chilham
Aylesham
Snowdown

A

KENT

Selling Tun.

Hothfield–Tarmac
Stone Term.
Wye
Powell
Duffryn
Coal
Dep.
C.S.
CE Depot
AF
Ashford
C.S.
Crane Repair Shops - M & EE
Isis Link
Wheel
Shops-
M & EE

Folkstone
Warren*

Dollands
Moor Sidings
Cheriton
Shuttle Terminal
Sandling
East*
Martello
Tun.
Westenhanger
West   Cen.
Sandling Tun.
Saltwood
Tunnel
Hythe
C.S.
Harbour
FOLKESTONE

Staplehurst
Headcorn
Pluckley
Marden

12

Ham Street

Tenterden
Town
Rolvenden
*KENT & EAST
SUSSEX RAILWAY*
Hexden
Bridge
Wittersham
Road
Appledore
Northiam
Bodiam   *Dixter*
Robertsbridge
Mountfield Tun.
Mountfield
Siding

B

Burmarsh Road Halt*
Dymchurch
*ROMNEY, HYTHE &
DYMCHURCH RAILWAY*
(1' 3")
Jefferstone Lane
New Romney

**EAST
SUSSEX**

Rye
Winchelsea
Doleham
Battle
Crowhurst
Three Oaks
Ore Tun.
West St.
Leonards
*Hastings
Tun.* C.S.
Ore
Mount Pleasant Tun.
Hastings
St. Leonards Warrior Sq.
Bexhill
St. Leonards C.S. (SL)
*Bopeep
Junc.
& Tun.*
Galley Hill-
Hydleman

Greatstone Halt
Romney Sands
Lade Halt
The Pilot Halt
Dungeness
Nuclear P.S.
Dungeness

C

1

2

0   5   10 m.
(1:350,000)
0   5   10   15 km.

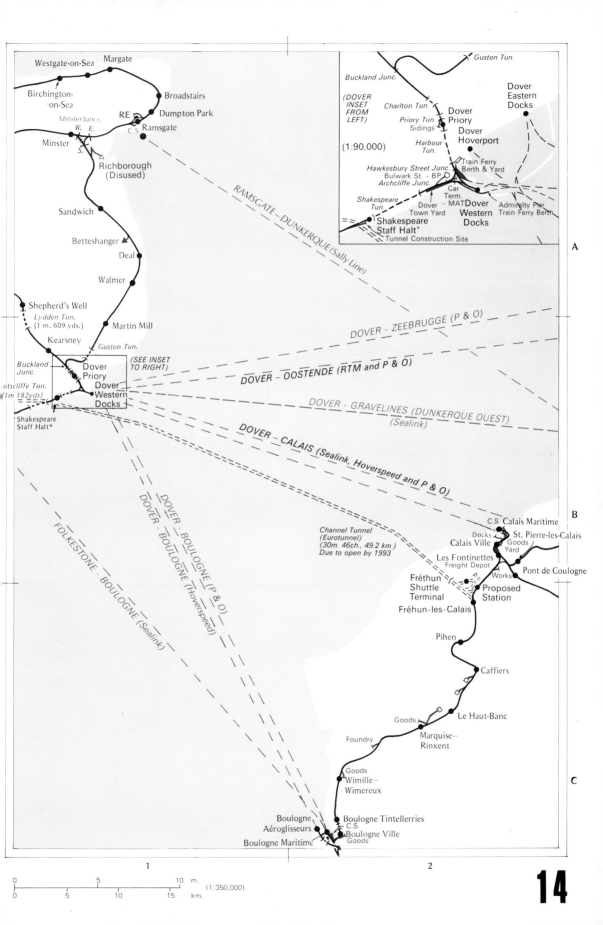

Westgate-on-Sea Margate
Birchington-on-Sea
Broadstairs
RE Dumpton Park
Minster Juncs. C.S. Ramsgate
W. E.
Minster
S.
Richborough
(Disused)
Sandwich
Betteshanger
Deal
Walmer
Shepherd's Well
Lydden Tun.
(1 m. 609 yds.) Martin Mill
Kearsney
Guston Tun.
Buckland Dover (SEE INSET
Junc. Priory TO RIGHT)
otscliffe Tun. Dover
(1m 182yds.) Western
Docks
Shakespeare
Staff Halt*

RAMSGATE – DUNKERQUE (Sally Line)

DOVER – ZEEBRUGGE (P & O)

DOVER – OOSTENDE (RTM and P & O)

DOVER – GRAVELINES (DUNKERQUE OUEST)
(Sealink)

DOVER – CALAIS (Sealink, Hoverspeed and P & O)

FOLKESTONE – BOULOGNE (Sealink)

DOVER – BOULOGNE (Hoverspeed)

DOVER – BOULOGNE (P & O)

Channel Tunnel
(Eurotunnel)
(30m. 46ch., 49.2 km.)
Due to open by 1993

C.S. Calais Maritime
Docks St. Pierre-les-Calais
Calais Ville Goods
Yard
Les Fontinettes Works
Freight Depot Pont de Coulogne
Fréthun Proposed
Shuttle Station
Terminal
Fréhun-les-Calais
Pihen
Caffiers
Goods Le Haut-Banc
Foundry Marquise–
Rinxent
Goods
Wimille–
Wimereux
Boulogne Boulogne Tintellerries
Aéroglisseurs C.S.
Boulogne Ville
Boulogne Maritime Goods

Inset (Dover)

Guston Tun.
Buckland Junc.
(DOVER Charlton Tun. Dover
INSET Priory
FROM Priory Tun. Dover
LEFT) Sidings Hoverport
(1:90,000) Harbour
Tun.
Hawkesbury Street Junc. Train Ferry
Bulwark St. – B.P.O. Berth & Yard
Archcliffe Junc. Car
Term.
Shakespeare Dover – MAT Dover
Tun. Dover Western
Town Yard Docks
Shakespeare Admiralty Pier
Staff Halt* Train Ferry Berth
Tunnel Construction Site

Dover Eastern Docks

A

B

C

0   5   10 m.
0   5   10   15 km.
(1:350,000)

1   2

14

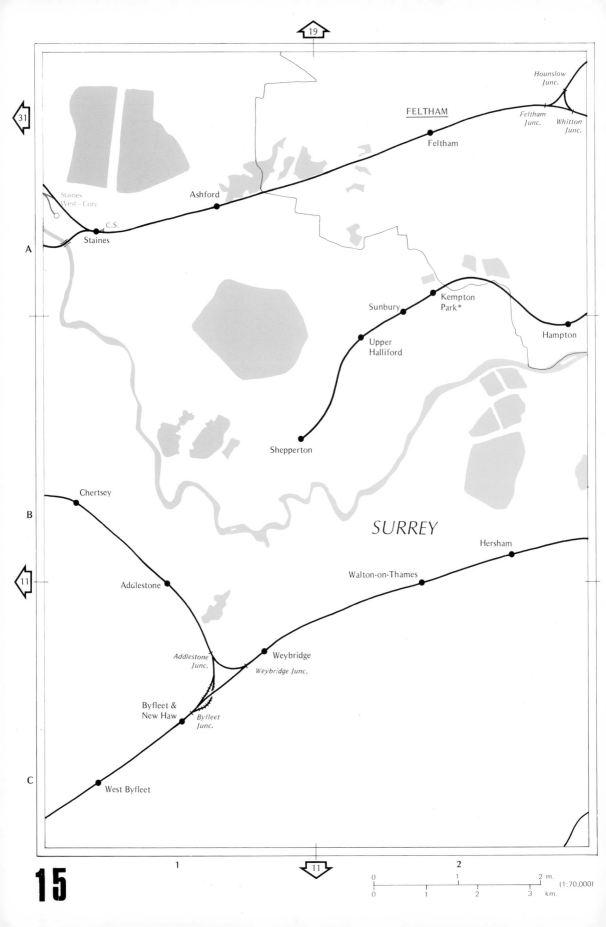

31

FELTHAM

Hounslow
Junc.

Feltham
Junc.

Whitton
Junc.

Feltham

Staines
West – Cory

Ashford

C.S.

A

Staines

Sunbury

Kempton
Park*

Upper
Halliford

Hampton

Shepperton

Chertsey

B

SURREY

Hersham

Walton-on-Thames

11

Addlestone

Addlestone
Junc.

Weybridge

Weybridge Junc.

Byfleet &
New Haw

Byfleet
Junc.

C

West Byfleet

15

1

2

0   1   2 m.

0   1   2   3   km.

(1:70,000)

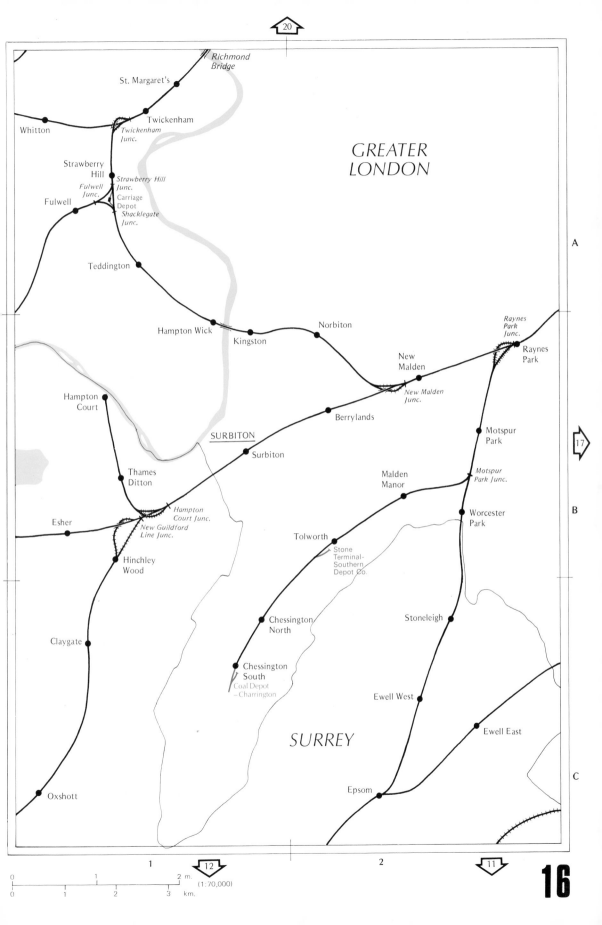

Richmond
Bridge

St. Margaret's

Twickenham

Whitton

*Twickenham
Junc.*

GREATER
LONDON

Strawberry
Hill

*Strawberry Hill
Junc.*

*Fulwell
Junc.*

Fulwell

Carriage
Depot

*Shacklegate
Junc.*

A

Teddington

Raynes
Park
Junc.

Norbiton

Hampton Wick

Kingston

New
Malden

Raynes
Park

Hampton
Court

Berrylands

*New Malden
Junc.*

SURBITON

Motspur
Park

17

Surbiton

Thames
Ditton

Malden
Manor

*Motspur
Park Junc.*

B

Esher

*Hampton
Court Junc.*

*New Guildford
Line Junc.*

Tolworth

Worcester
Park

Hinchley
Wood

Stone
Terminal-
Southern
Depot Co.

Claygate

Stoneleigh

Chessington
North

Chessington
South

Coal Depot
– Charrington

Ewell West

Ewell East

SURREY

Oxshott

Epsom

C

D

East Putney Tun.

Southfields

Wandsworth Common

Clapham South

Balham

C.S. & E.M.U. Depot

Herne Hill N. Junc.

Herne Hill

S. Junc.

North Dulwich

Earlsfield

D

Streatham Hill

Tulse Hill

Knight's Hill Tunnel

West Dulwich

WD

Balham Junc.

N

Tooting Bec

Leigham Junc.

West Norwood Junc.

Sydenham Hill

Wimbledon Park

Wimbledon Staff Halt*

Leigham Court (Streatham Hill) Tun.

West Norwood

WIMBLEDON (Under construction)

Tooting Broadway

Leigham Tun.

Penge Tunnel (1 m. 381 yds)

A

Haydons Road

Tooting

Streatham Junc. North

Streatham

Streatham Tun.

Gipsy Hill

Crystal Palace Tun.

'A' Junc.

Wimbledon

Collier's Wood

Streatham Junc. S.

Streatham Junc.

'B' Junc.

Wimbledon S & T Depot

Streatham Common

Crystal Palace

'C' Junc.

Merton Park

South Wimbledon

Morden Road

Streatham Common Junc.

Norbury

Bromley Junc.

Wimbledon Chase

N

GREATER LONDON

South Merton

Morden

Thornton Heath

Norwood Junction

Norwood Junc.

Depot

Selhurst Depot (SU)

Norwood Fork Junc.

Morden South

Mitcham

Mitcham Junction

Selhurst

16

Mitcham North Junc.

Beddington Lane

Selhurst Junc.

Gloucester Rd. Junc.

Norwood Yard

St. Helier

Mitcham South Junc.

Cottage Junc.

Windmill Bridge Junc.

Depot

B

Hackbridge

Waddon Marsh

West Croydon

Addiscombe

Sutton Common

East Croydon

Carshalton

Waddon

West Sutton

South Croydon

Sanderstead

Sutton Junc.

Sutton

Wallington

South Croydon Junc.

Selsdon – Cory

Sutton Wimbledon Line Junc.

Carshalton Beeches

Selsdon Junc.

Cheam

Purley Oaks

Belmont

Coal Depot-Charrington

Purley

Caterham Line Junc.

Stone Terminal – Brett Marine

Riddlesdown

C

Reedham

Chipstead Line Junc.

Riddlesdown Tunnel

SURREY

Kenley

Banstead

17

B	BAKERLOO	M	METROPOLITAN
C	CENTRAL	M(EL)	METROPOLITAN (East London)
O	CIRCLE	N	NORTHERN
D	DISTRICT	P	PICCADILLY
J	JUBILEE	V	VICTORIA

1

2

0 .... 1 .... 2 m.

0 ...... 1 ...... 2 ...... 3 km.

(1:70,000)

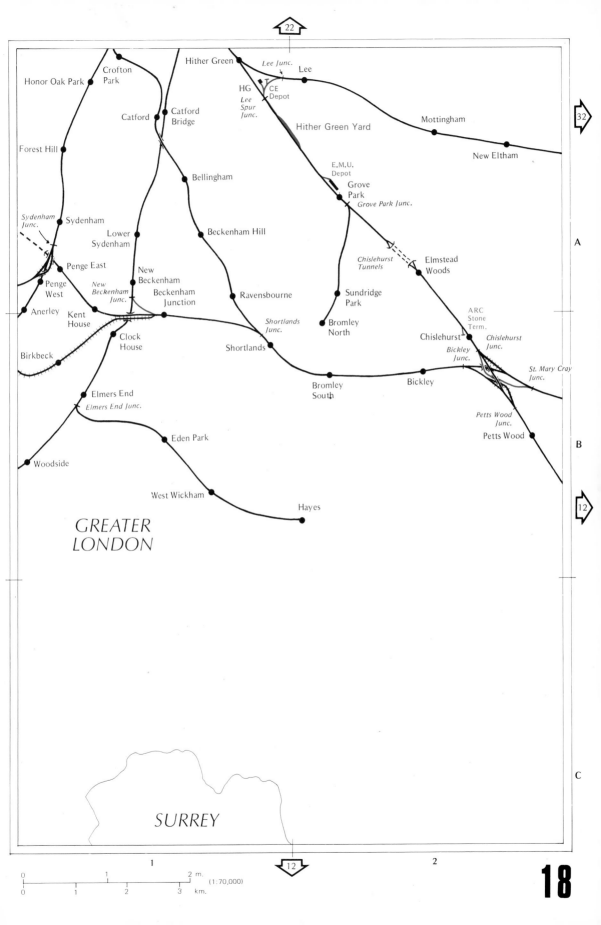

Honor Oak Park

Crofton Park

Hither Green

22

Lee Junc.

Lee

HG
Lee Spur Junc.

CE Depot

Hither Green Yard

Mottingham

32

Catford

Catford Bridge

New Eltham

Forest Hill

Bellingham

E.M.U. Depot

Grove Park

Grove Park Junc.

Sydenham Junc.

Sydenham

Beckenham Hill

A

Lower Sydenham

Chislehurst Tunnels

Elmstead Woods

Penge East

New Beckenham

Ravensbourne

Penge West

New Beckenham Junc.

Beckenham Junction

Sundridge Park

ARC Stone Term.

Anerley

Kent House

Shortlands Junc.

Bromley North

Chislehurst

Chislehurst Junc.

Bickley Junc.

Clock House

Shortlands

St. Mary Cray Junc.

Birkbeck

Elmers End

Elmers End Junc.

Bromley South

Bickley

Petts Wood Junc.

Eden Park

Petts Wood

B

Woodside

West Wickham

Hayes

12

GREATER LONDON

C

SURREY

0   1   2 m.
0   1   2   3   km.
(1:70,000)

1

12

2

18

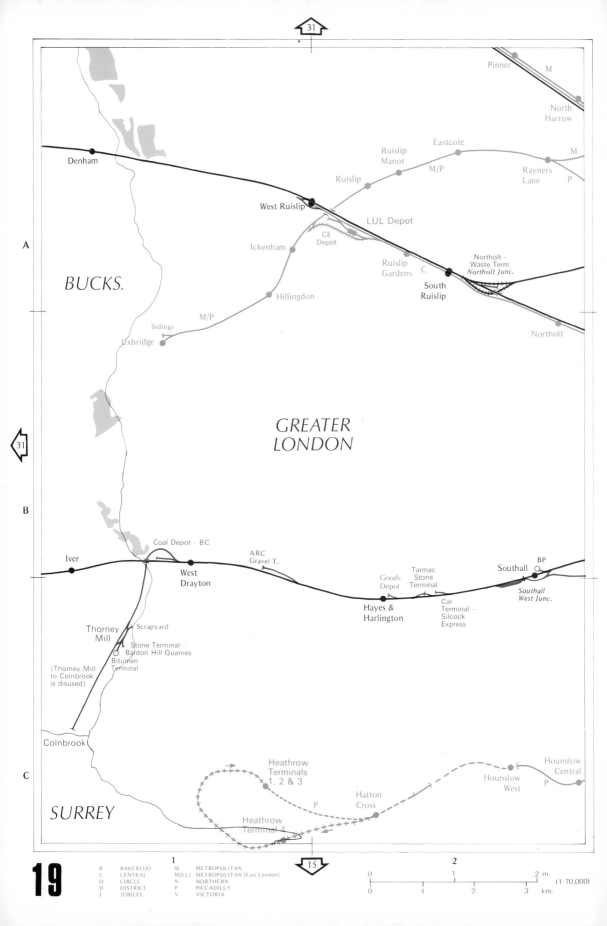

Pinner
M
North
Harrow
Denham
Eastcote
Ruislip
Manor
M/P
Rayners
Lane
M
Ruislip
P
West Ruislip
LUL Depot
CE
Depot
Northolt –
Waste Term.
Northolt Junc.
Ruislip
Gardens
C
South
Ruislip

A
Ickenham
Northolt

BUCKS.
Hillingdon
Sidings
M/P
Uxbridge

GREATER
LONDON

B
Iver
Coal Depot – BC
ARC
Gravel T.
West
Drayton
Goods
Depot
Tarmac
Stone
Terminal
Southall
BP
*Southall
West Junc.*
Hayes &
Harlington
Car
Terminal –
Silcock
Express

Thorney
Mill
Scrapyard
Stone Terminal –
Bardon Hill Quarries
Bitumen
Terminal
(Thorney Mill
to Colnbrook
is disused)

Colnbrook

Heathrow
Terminals
1, 2 & 3
Hounslow
Central
P
Hounslow
West
Hatton
Cross
P
C
SURREY
Heathrow
Terminal 4

19

B	BAKERLOO	1	M	METROPOLITAN
C	CENTRAL		M(EL)	METROPOLITAN (East London)
O	CIRCLE		N	NORTHERN
D	DISTRICT		P	PICCADILLY
J	JUBILEE		V	VICTORIA

0		1			2 m.	
						(1:70,000)
0	1	2	3	km.		

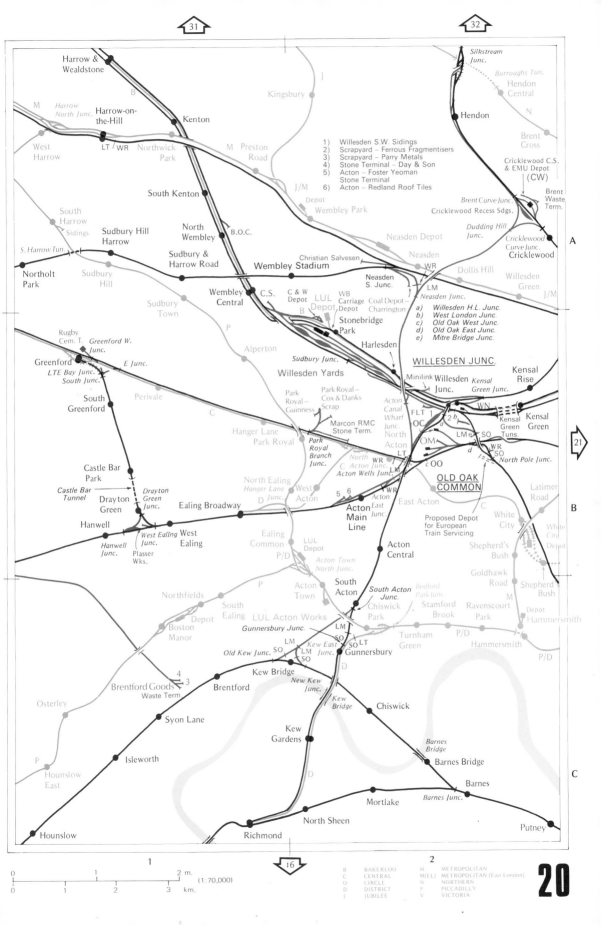

a) Belsize Fast Tun. (1m 11yd).
b) Belsize Slow Tun. (1m 107yd).
c) Smithfield Tun.
d) Snow Hill Tun.
e) Camden Road. E. Junc.
f) S. Tottenham W. Junc.
g) S. Tottenham E. Junc.
h) Tottenham S. Junc.
j) Ludgate Hill Junc.
k) Camden Road Junc.
l) Blackfriars Junc.
m) Metropolitan Junc.
n) Stoney St. Junc.
p) Borough Market Junc.
q) Freight Terminal Junc.
r) Dock Junc.
s) Tottenham N. Cve. No. 1 Tun.
t) Tottenham N. Cve. No. 2 Tun.
u) Tottenham N. Cve. No. 3 Tun.

1) Aldgate
2) Temple
3) St. Paul's
4) Monument
5) Mansion House
6) Embankment
7) Piccadilly Circus
8) Warren Street
9) Churchyard C.S.
10) EMU Depot
11) Stew. La. – RMC Stone T.
12) W. District Office
13) W. Cen. District Office
14) Mount Pleasant Sort. Off.
15) E. Cen. District Office

LIVERPOOL ST. (Under construction)

(Dockland extension to Bank is under construction)

(SEE INSET PAGE 22)

KING'S CROSS   LIVERPOOL ST.

EUSTON   VICTORIA

East Finchley, Highgate, Golders Green, Hampstead Heath, Gospel Oak, Tufnell Park, Kentish Town, Camden Town, King's Cross, Finsbury Park, Arsenal, Hornsey, Harringay, Crouch Hill, Manor House, Seven Sisters, South Tottenham, Stamford Hill, Stoke Newington, Rectory Road, Tottenham Hale

West Hampstead, Finchley Rd. & Frognal, Kilburn, Brondesbury, Brondesbury Park, Queen's Park, Kilburn High Rd., Swiss Cottage, St. John's Wood, Maida Vale, Westbourne Park, Royal Oak, Paddington, Warwick Ave., Ladbroke Grove, Notting Hill Gate, Holland Park, Queensway, Bayswater, Lancaster Gate, Marble Arch, Bond St., Marylebone, Edgware Rd., Baker St., Regents Pk., Gt. Portland St., Euston Sq., Warren St., Russell Sq., Goodge St., Tott. Ct. Rd., Oxford Circus, Leicester Sq., Covent Gdn., Holborn, Chancery Lane, Farringdon, Barbican, Moorgate, Old Street, Angel, Bank, Aldgate East, Fenchurch St., Tower Hill, Tower Gateway, London Bridge

Kensington Olympia, Barons Court, West Kensington, Earl's Court, West Brompton, Fulham Broadway, Parsons Green, Putney Bridge, East Putney, Wandsworth Town, Clapham Junction, High St. Kensington, Gloucester Rd., South Kensington, Sloane Square, Victoria, Hyde Park Corner, Green Park, Knightsbridge, St. James's Park, Westminster, Charing Cross, Waterloo, Embankment, Blackfriars, Cannon St., Temple, Aldwych, Holborn Viaduct, Pimlico, Vauxhall, Oval, Stockwell, Kennington, Elephant & Castle, Borough, Lambeth North, Battersea, Queenstown Rd., Wandsworth Road, Clapham, Clapham North, Brixton, Loughborough Junction, Denmark Hill, Peckham Rye, East Dulwich, Grove

B BAKERLOO
C CENTRAL
D CIRCLE
DL DOCKLAND
J JUBILEE
M METROPOLITAN
M(EL) METROPOLITAN (East London)
N NORTHERN
P PICCADILLY
V VICTORIA

0 ... 1 ... 2 m.
0 ... 1 ... 2 ... 3 km.
(1:70,000)

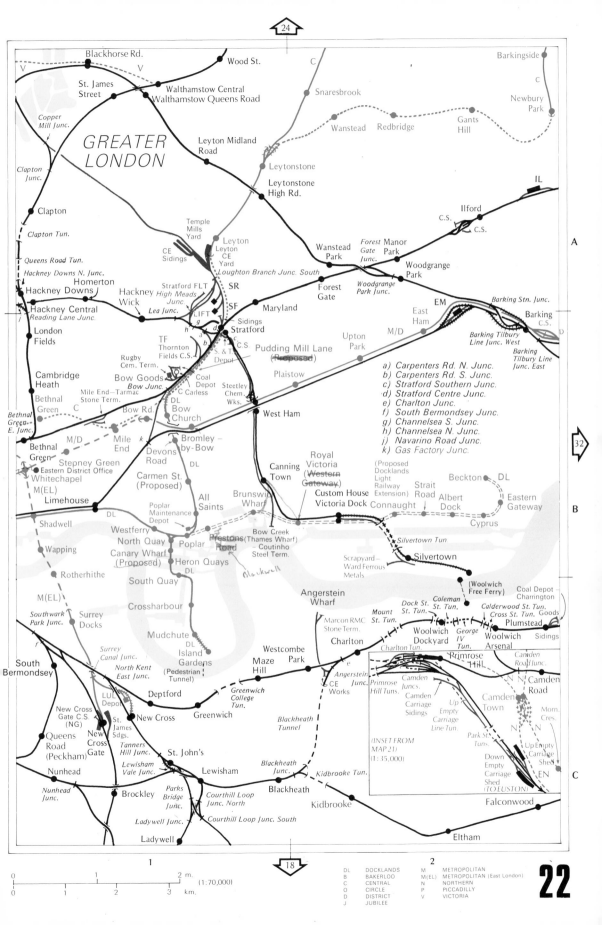

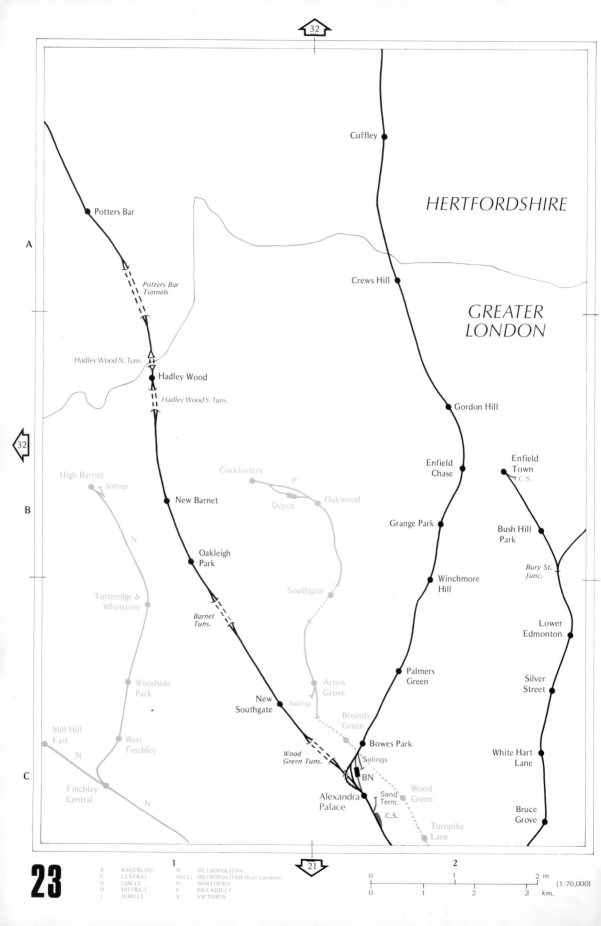

Cuffley

HERTFORDSHIRE

Potters Bar

A

Crews Hill

GREATER LONDON

Potters Bar
Tunnels

Hadley Wood N. Tuns.

Hadley Wood

Gordon Hill

Hadley Wood S. Tuns.

32

Enfield
Chase

Enfield
Town
C.S.

High Barnet   Cockfosters   P

Sidings

B   New Barnet   Depot   Oakwood

Grange Park

Bush Hill
Park

N

Oakleigh
Park

Winchmore
Hill

Bury St.
Junc.

Totteridge &
Whetstone

Barnet
Tuns.

Southgate

Lower
Edmonton

Woodside
Park

Palmers
Green

Silver
Street

Mill Hill
East

West
Finchley

New
Southgate

Arnos
Grove

Sidings

Bounds
Green

N

Bowes Park

Sidings

White Hart
Lane

C

Finchley
Central

N

Wood
Green Tuns.

BN

Wood
Green

Bruce
Grove

Alexandra
Palace

Sand
Term.

C.S.

Turnpike
Lane

23

B	BAKERLOO	M	METROPOLITAN
C	CENTRAL	M(EL)	METROPOLITAN (East London)
O	CIRCLE	N	NORTHERN
D	DISTRICT	P	PICCADILLY
I	JUBILEE	V	VICTORIA

0   1   2 m.

0   1   2   3   km.

(1:70,000)

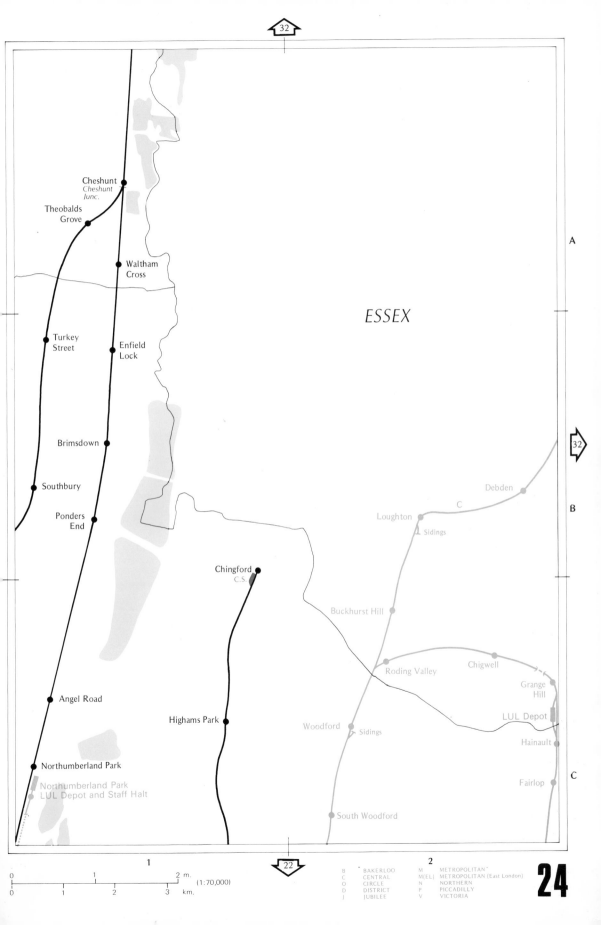

Cheshunt
Cheshunt Junc.

Theobalds
Grove

Waltham
Cross

ESSEX

Turkey
Street

Enfield
Lock

Brimsdown

Debden

Loughton

C

A

B

Southbury

Ponders
End

Chingford
C.S.

⊥ Sidings

Buckhurst Hill

Roding Valley

Chigwell

Grange
Hill

LUL Depot

Angel Road

Highams Park

Woodford

Sidings

Hainault

Northumberland Park

Northumberland Park
LUL Depot and Staff Halt

South Woodford

Fairlop

C

1   2

0   1   2 m.   (1:70,000)
0   1   2   3   km.

B	BAKERLOO	M	METROPOLITAN
C	CENTRAL	M(EL)	METROPOLITAN (East London)
C	CIRCLE	N	NORTHERN
D	DISTRICT	P	PICCADILLY
J	JUBILEE	V	VICTORIA

24

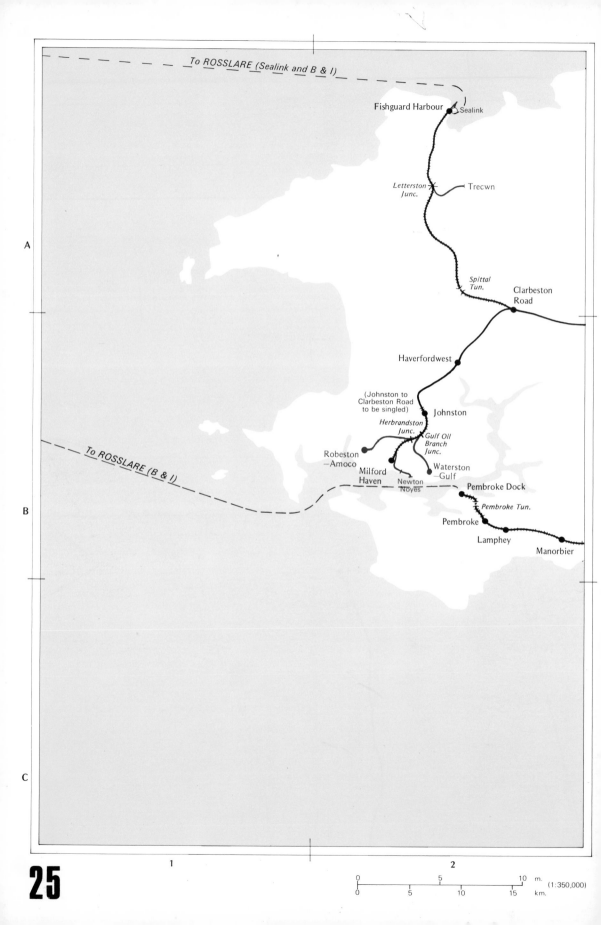

To ROSSLARE (Sealink and B & I)

Fishguard Harbour ● Sealink

Letterston Junc. ✕ ── Trecwn

Spittal Tun.

Clarbeston Road ●

Haverfordwest ●

(Johnston to Clarbeston Road to be singled)

Johnston ●

Herbrandston Junc.

Gulf Oil Branch Junc.

Robeston —Amoco

Milford Haven

Newton Noyes

Waterston —Gulf

To ROSSLARE (B & I)

Pembroke Dock ●

Pembroke Tun.

Pembroke ●

Lamphey ●

Manorbier ●

A

B

C

1

2

0 ─ 5 ─ 10 m.
0 ─ 5 ─ 10 ─ 15 km.

(1:350,000)

25

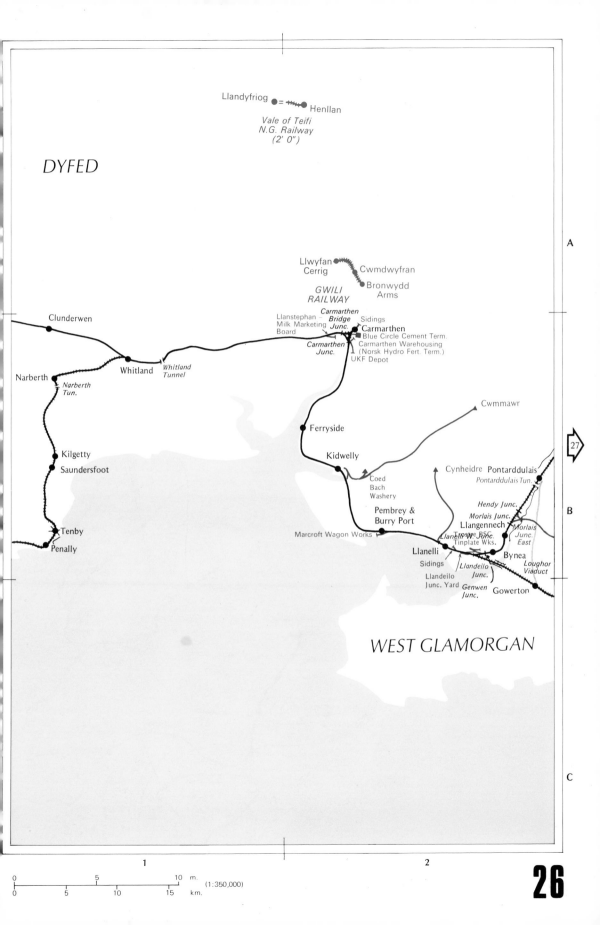

Llandyfriog ● = ✦✦✦ ● Henllan

Vale of Teifi
N.G. Railway
(2' 0")

DYFED

Llwyfan ●✦✦✦
Cerrig ✦✦ Cwmdwyfran
✦✦
GWILI ● Bronwydd
RAILWAY Arms

Clunderwen
                                    Carmarthen
                    Llanstephan ~ *Bridge* Sidings
                    Milk Marketing *Junc.* Carmarthen
Narberth   Board   ● Blue Circle Cement Term.
                                    Carmarthen ⊥ Carmarthen Warehousing
         Whitland *Whitland*   *Junc.* (Norsk Hydro Fert. Term.)
         Narberth *Tunnel*   UKF Depot
         Tun.

                                                              Cwmmawr ▲

Kilgetty   ● Ferryside
Saundersfoot
                            Kidwelly   Cynheidre Pontarddulais
                                                  ▲   *Pontarddulais Tun.*
                              Coed
                              Bach   *Hendy Junc.*
Tenby   Washery   *Morlais Junc.*
Penally   Pembrey &   Llangennech *Morlais*
                    Marcroft Wagon Works Burry Port   *Junc.*
                                                 Llanelli West Junc. *East*
                                                   Tinplate Wks.
                                       Llanelli   ═ Bynea
                                       Sidings   *Loughor*
                                              Llandeilo   *Viaduct*
                                       Llandeilo *Junc.*
                                       Junc. Yard *Genwen* Gowerton
                                                   Junc.

WEST GLAMORGAN

A

27

B

C

1   2

0   5   10 m.   (1:350,000)
0   5   10   15   km.

26

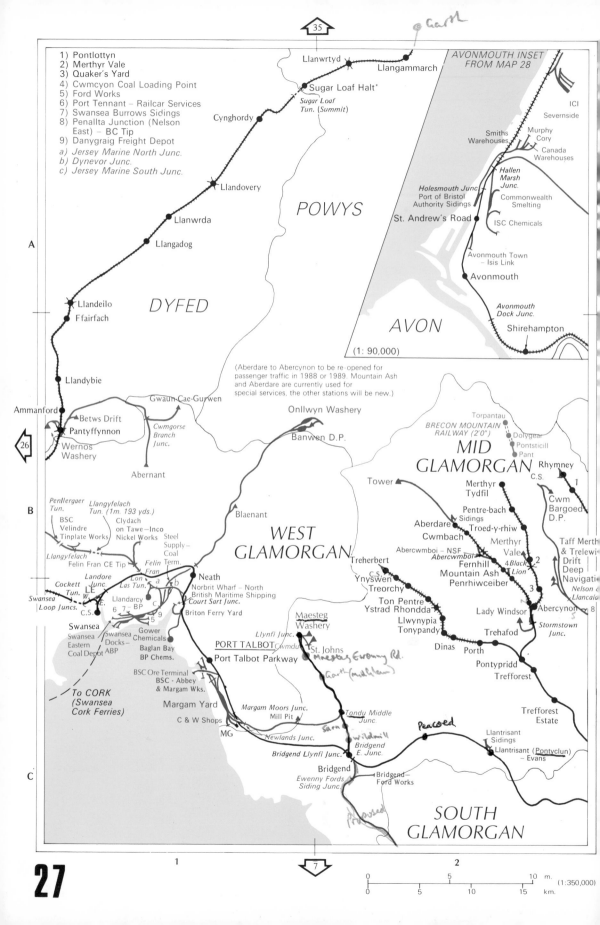

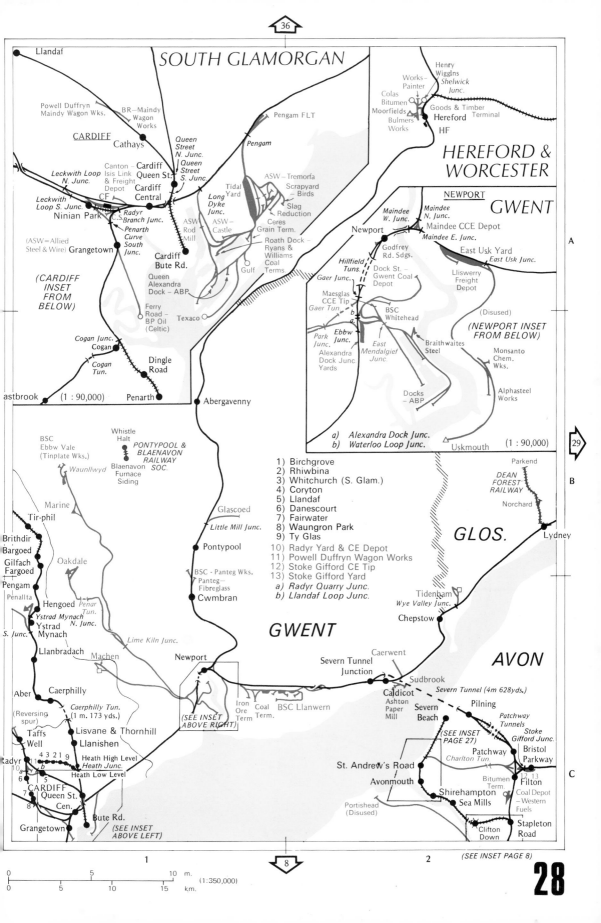

SOUTH GLAMORGAN

Llandaf

Powell Duffryn
Maindy Wagon Wks.

BR—Maindy
Wagon Works

CARDIFF
Cathays

Pengam FLT

Pengam

Queen
Street
N. Junc.

Queen
Street
S. Junc.

Cardiff
Queen St.

Canton
Isis Link
& Freight
Depot

Leckwith Loop
N. Junc.

Cardiff
Central

CF

Leckwith
Loop S. Junc.

Ninian Park

Radyr
Branch Junc.

C.S.

Penarth
Curve
South
Junc.

Grangetown

(ASW = Allied
Steel & Wire)

Cardiff
Bute Rd.

Queen
Alexandra
Dock – ABP.

Ferry
Road –
BP Oil
(Celtic)

Long
Dyke
Junc.

ASW –
Castle

ASW –
Rod Mill

ASW – Tremorfa
Scrapyard
– Birds

Slag
Reduction

Ceres
Grain Term.

Roath Dock –
Ryans &
Williams
Coal
Terms.

Gulf

Texaco

Tidal
Yard

(CARDIFF
INSET
FROM
BELOW)

astbrook

(1 : 90,000)

Cogan Junc.

Cogan

Cogan Tun.

Dingle
Road

Penarth

Abergavenny

BSC
Ebbw Vale
(Tinplate Wks.)

Whistle
Halt

Waunllwyd

PONTYPOOL &
BLAENAVON
RAILWAY
SOC.

Blaenavon
Furnace
Siding

Marine

Glascoed

Tir-phil

Little Mill Junc.

Brithdir
Bargoed
Gilfach
Fargoed
Pengam

Oakdale

Pontypool

Penallta

Hengoed

Penar
Tun.

BSC - Panteg Wks.

Panteg –
Fibreglass

Cwmbran

Ystrad Mynach
N. Junc.

Ystrad
Mynach

S. Junc.

Lime Kiln Junc.

Llanbradach

Machen

Newport

GWENT

Aber

Caerphilly

Caerphilly Tun.
(1 m. 173 yds.)

(Reversing
spur)

Taffs
Well

Lisvane &
Llanishen
Thornhill

(SEE INSET
ABOVE RIGHT)

Iron Ore
Term.

Coal
Term.

BSC Llanwern

Radyr

4 3 2 1 9

10

a

b

6

5

7

CARDIFF
Queen St.
Cen.

8

Grangetown

Bute Rd.

(SEE INSET
ABOVE LEFT)

Heath High Level
Heath Junc.
Heath Low Level

HEREFORD &
WORCESTER

Henry
Wiggins
Shelwick
Junc.

Works –
Painter

Colas
Bitumen
Moorfields
Bulmers
Works

Goods & Timber
Terminal

Hereford

HF

NEWPORT

GWENT

Maindee
W. Junc.

Maindee
N. Junc.

Maindee CCE Depot

Newport

Maindee E. Junc.

Godfrey
Rd. Sdgs.

East Usk Yard

East Usk Junc.

Hillfield
Tuns.

Gaer Junc.

Dock St. –
Gwent Coal
Depot

Llisworry
Freight
Depot

Maesglas
CCE Tip

Gaer Tun.

b

Park
Junc.

Ebbw
Junc.

a

BSC
Whitehead

(Disused)

(NEWPORT INSET
FROM BELOW)

Braithwaites
Steel

Monsanto
Chem.
Wks.

Alexandra
Dock Junc.
Yards

East
Mendalgief
Junc.

Docks
– ABP.

Alphasteel
Works

Uskmouth

a) Alexandra Dock Junc.
b) Waterloo Loop Junc.

(1 : 90,000)

GWENT

A

DEAN
FOREST
RAILWAY

Parkend

Norchard

GLOS.

Lydney

Tidenham

Wye Valley Junc.

Chepstow

AVON

B

1) Birchgrove
2) Rhiwbina
3) Whitchurch (S. Glam.)
4) Coryton
5) Llandaf
6) Danescourt
7) Fairwater
8) Waungron Park
9) Ty Glas
10) Radyr Yard & CE Depot
11) Powell Duffryn Wagon Works
12) Stoke Gifford CE Tip
13) Stoke Gifford Yard
a) Radyr Quarry Junc.
b) Llandaf Loop Junc.

Severn Tunnel
Junction

Caerwent

Sudbrook

Caldicot
Ashton
Paper
Mill

Severn Tunnel (4m 628yds.)

Severn
Beach

Pilning

Patchway
Tunnels

Stoke
Gifford Junc.

(SEE INSET
PAGE 27)

St. Andrew's Road

Avonmouth

Patchway

Charlton Tun.

Bitumen
Term.

Bristol
Parkway

12-13

Filton

Coal Depot
– Western
Fuels

Shirehampton

Sea Mills

Portishead
(Disused)

Clifton
Down

Stapleton
Road

C

1

2

(SEE INSET PAGE 8)

0   5   10 m.
0   5   10   15 km.

(1:350,000)

29

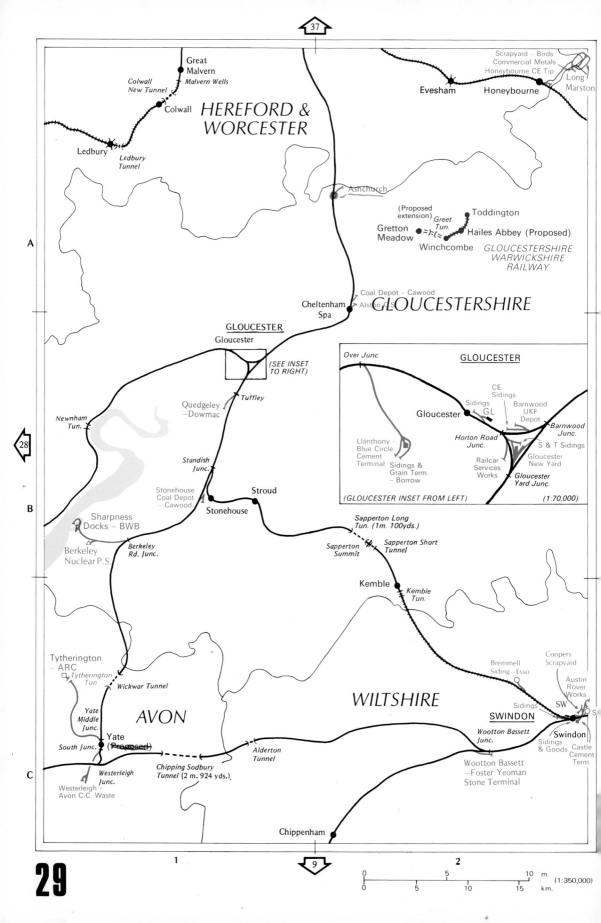

Great
Malvern
Colwall
New Tunnel ·· *Malvern Wells*
Colwall

HEREFORD &
WORCESTER

Evesham Honeybourne

Scrapyard – Birds
Commercial Metals
Honeybourne CE Tip

Long
Marston

Ledbury
Ledbury
Tunnel

Ashchurch

(Proposed
extension) *Greet*
Tun.
Gretton
Meadow

Toddington

Hailes Abbey (Proposed)

Winchcombe

GLOUCESTERSHIRE
WARWICKSHIRE
RAILWAY

Coal Depot – Cawood
Cheltenham Alston C.S.
Spa

GLOUCESTERSHIRE

GLOUCESTER

Gloucester

(SEE INSET
TO RIGHT)

Quedgeley
—Dowmac

Tuffley

Newnham
Tun.

Standish
Junc.

Stonehouse Coal Depot
– Cawood

Stroud

Stonehouse

GLOUCESTER INSET

Over Junc.

Gloucester

CE
Sidings

Sidings
GL

Barnwood
UKF
Depot

Horton Road
Junc.

Barnwood
Junc.

Llanthony –
Blue Circle
Cement
Terminal

Sidings &
Grain Term.
– Borrow

S & T Sidings

Railcar
Services
Works

Gloucester
New Yard

Gloucester
Yard Junc.

(GLOUCESTER INSET FROM LEFT)

(1:70,000)

Sharpness
Docks – BWB

Sapperton Long
Tun. (1m. 100yds.)

Sapperton
Summit

Sapperton Short
Tunnel

Berkeley
Rd. Junc.

Berkeley
Nuclear P.S.

Kemble

Kemble
Tun.

Tytherington
– ARC
Tytherington
Tun

Wickwar Tunnel

WILTSHIRE

Bremmell
Siding – Esso

Coopers
Scrapyard

Austin
Rover
Works

Yate
Middle
Junc.

Yate
(Proposed)

AVON

South Junc.

SW

Sidings

SWINDON

Swindon

Wootton Bassett
Junc.

Sidings
& Goods

Castle
Cement
Term.

Alderton
Tunnel

Westerleigh
Junc.

Westerleigh –
Avon C.C. Waste

Chipping Sodbury
Tunnel (2 m. 924 yds.)

Wootton Bassett
—Foster Yeoman
Stone Terminal

Chippenham

1

2

0   5   10   m.
0   5   10   15   km.

(1:350,000)

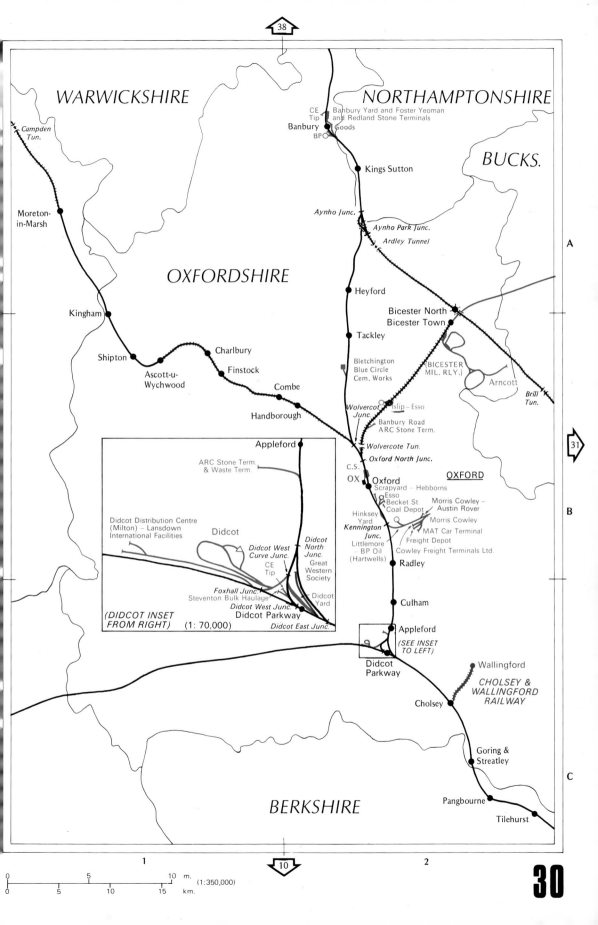

WARWICKSHIRE

NORTHAMPTONSHIRE

BUCKS.

CE Tip Banbury Yard and Foster Yeoman
and Redland Stone Terminals
Banbury Goods
BPO

Kings Sutton

A

Campden Tun.

Moreton-in-Marsh

OXFORDSHIRE

Aynho Junc.

Aynho Park Junc.
Ardley Tunnel

Heyford

Bicester North
Bicester Town

Kingham

Tackley

(BICESTER MIL. RLY.)

Arncott

Brill Tun.

Charlbury

Shipton

Finstock

Bletchington
Blue Circle
Cem. Works

Ascott-u-Wychwood

Combe

Islip – Esso
Wolvercot Junc.
Banbury Road
ARC Stone Term.

31

Handborough

Wolvercote Tun.

Appleford

Oxford North Junc.

C.S.
OX

Oxford

OXFORD

Scrapyard – Hebborns
Esso
Becket St.
Coal Depot

Morris Cowley –
Austin Rover

B

ARC Stone Term.
& Waste Term.

Hinksey
Yard

Morris Cowley

Kennington Junc.

MAT Car Terminal
Freight Depot

Littlemore
– BP Oil
(Hartwells)

Cowley Freight Terminals Ltd.

Didcot Distribution Centre
(Milton) – Lansdown
International Facilities

Didcot

Didcot West Curve Junc.

Didcot North Junc.

Radley

CE Tip

Great Western Society

Culham

Foxhall Junc.
Steventon Bulk Haulage

Didcot West Junc.
Didcot Parkway

Didcot Yard

Appleford

(SEE INSET TO LEFT)

(DIDCOT INSET FROM RIGHT) (1: 70,000)

Didcot East Junc.

Didcot Parkway

Wallingford

CHOLSEY &
WALLINGFORD
RAILWAY

Cholsey

Goring &
Streatley

C

BERKSHIRE

Pangbourne

Tilehurst

1

2

0   5   10 m.
| | | | | | | | | (1:350,000)
0   5   10   15 km.

30

Wolverton
Transport & Warehousing Facilities Ltd.
ARC Stone Terminal
BRML (ZN)

Kempston Hardwick
Forders Sidings
London Brick Wks.
Stewartby
Millbrook CE Tip
Lidlington

Elstow – Redland Stone Terminal
Biggleswade

Plasmor Brick Terminal

BEDFORDSHIRE

Milton Keynes Central
BLETCHLEY C.S.
Bletchley

Denbigh Hall South Junc.
BY
Fenny Stratford
Bow Brickhill
Fenny Stratford Flyover Junc.
Bletchley Flyover Junc.
WR Stone Term. – Peakstone and Redland Roof Tiles

Woburn Sands
Ridgmont
Aspley Guise

Ampthill Tuns.

Flitwick

Harlington

Arlesey (Proposed)

CE Sidings
Hitchin
Cambridge Junc.
CE Yard

1) Headstone Lane
2) Harrow & Wealdstone
3) Croxley Green
4) Watford West
5) Mill Hill Broadway
6) Watford High Street
7) Watford Stadium*

Winslow*

Claydon L.N.E. Junc.
Calvert – GLC Waste Terminal

Linslade Tuns.
Leighton Buzzard

LEIGHTON BUZZARD N.G. RLY. (2' 0")

Blue Circle Cem. Term.
BP

Dunstable

Leagrave Sidings

Goods & Car Term.
Luton
Luton Bute St.

Grendon Underwood Junc.

Quainton Road*

Akeman Street – UKF Fertilizers

Cheddington

WHIPSNADE & UMFOLOZI RLY. (2' 6")

Pitstone (Tring Cutting) – Castle Cement Works

Tring Summit

Harpenden

Goods, Peakstone Terminal and Cawood Coal Depot
Aylesbury C.S.

Stoke Mandeville

Tring

Northchurch Tuns.
Berkhamsted

HERTFORDSHIRE

Haddenham and Thame Parkway

Little Kimble

Wendover

Thame – BP

Monks Risborough

Dutchlands Summit

Chesham
M

Hemel Hempstead

Parcels

St. Albans Abbey

St. Albans City
Newspapers Siding

Chinnor – Rugby Cement Works

Saunderton Summit

Princes Risborough

Great Missenden

Saunderton

(MANTLES WOOD)
LT

Chalfont & Latimer
WR
Amersham

Chorley Wood

Apsley

King's Langley
WATFORD JUNC.

Watford Slow Tun. (1m 230yds)
Watford Fast Tun. (1m 55yds)

Park St.

Bricket Wood

Stone Term. – Peakstone

Redland Aggr. Stone Term

Radlett

Garston
Watford North WJ
CE Sdgs.
Watford Junc.

8) Watford Cardiff Rd. P.S.
9) Reading CE Sidings
10) Queensbury
11) Kingsbury
12) Burnt Oak
13) Colindale
14) Canons Park

HIGH WYCOMBE (Proposed)

High Wycombe

Beaconsfield

Whitehouse Tun.

Seer Green

BUCKINGHAMSHIRE

Rickmansworth

Croxley C.S.M

Watford
Watford S. Junc.

8 A 6
3 4 7
Bushey

Watford Junc.

Elstree Tuns.

Carpenders Park

Hatch End

Stanmore
J 7 C.S.
14
2 10
N
11

Edgwa
5
12
13

(See Map)

Gerrards Cross

Denham Golf Club

Denham
West Ruislip
Pinner

Rayners Lane

Moor Park

Northwood

Northwood Hills

P

OXON.

Marlow

Cookham

Bourne End

Henley-on-Thames

Shiplake

Furze Platt

BERKSHIRE

Taplow

Burnham
Shell

SLOUGH

Slough

Langley Total

Uxbridge

GREATER LONDON

C

Ealing Bdy.

READING

Wargrave

Reading
9
RG
SO
Reading Spur Junc.
WR

Maidenhead
Car Term. (Disused)

Windsor & Eton Central
Windsor & Eton Riverside
Sunnymeads

Langley
Iver
West Drayton

Datchet

Heathrow Term. 4

Heathrow Term. 1, 2 & 3

(See Map 19)

P

Twyford

a) Reading West Junc.
b) Oxford Road Junc.
c) Reading New Junc.

Wraysbury

Feltham

Richmond

Reading West C.S.
a
b c

11

2

15

16

31

DL	DOCKLANDS	M	METROPOLITAN	
B	BAKERLOO	M(EL)	METROPOLITAN (East London)	
C	CENTRAL	N	NORTHERN	
O	CIRCLE	P	PICCADILLY	
D	DISTRICT	V	VICTORIA	
J	JUBILEE			

0 5 10 m.
0 5 10 15 km.
(1:350,000)

30

A

B

C

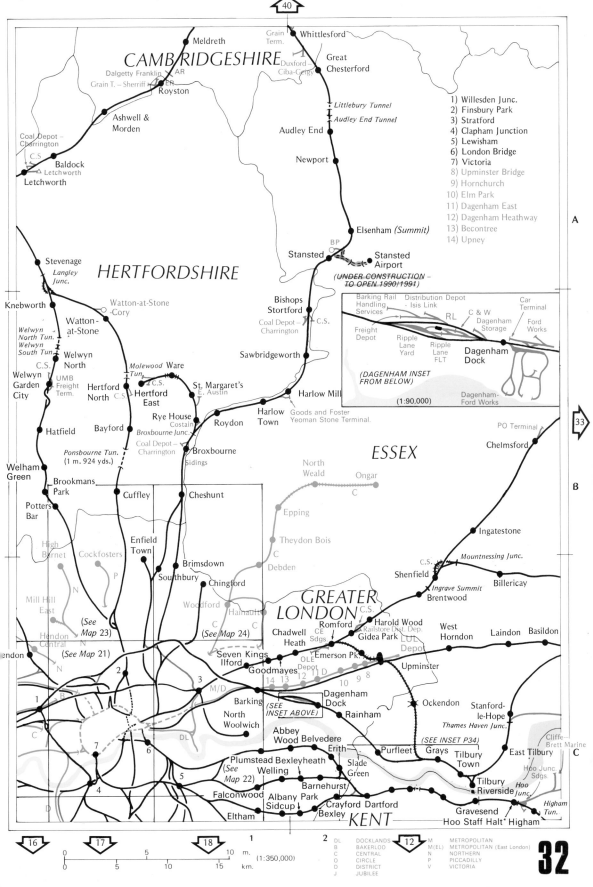

CAMBRIDGESHIRE

Meldreth
Whittlesford
Grain Term.
Duxford Ciba-Geigy
Great Chesterford
Dalgetty Franklin AR
Grain T. – Sherriff
Royston
Littlebury Tunnel
Audley End Tunnel
Ashwell & Morden
Coal Depot – Charrington
C.S.
Baldock
Letchworth
Letchworth
Audley End
Newport
Elsenham (Summit)

1) Willesden Junc.
2) Finsbury Park
3) Stratford
4) Clapham Junction
5) Lewisham
6) London Bridge
7) Victoria
8) Upminster Bridge
9) Hornchurch
10) Elm Park
11) Dagenham East
12) Dagenham Heathway
13) Becontree
14) Upney

A

Stevenage
Langley Junc.
HERTFORDSHIRE
Knebworth
Watton-at-Stone -Cory
Watton- at-Stone
Welwyn North Tun.
Welwyn South Tun.
C.S.
Welwyn Garden City
UMB Freight Term.
Welwyn North
Molewood Tun.
C.S.
Ware
Hertford North
C.S.
Hertford East
St. Margaret's
E. Austin
Hatfield
Bayford
Rye House
Costain
Roydon
Broxbourne Junc.
Coal Depot – Charrington
Broxbourne
Sidings
Welham Green
Ponsbourne Tun. (1 m. 924 yds.)
Brookmans Park
Cuffley
Cheshunt
Bishops Stortford
Coal Depot – Charrington
C.S.
Sawbridgeworth
Harlow Mill
Harlow Town
Goods and Foster Yeoman Stone Terminal.

Stansted
BP
Stansted Airport
(UNDER CONSTRUCTION – TO OPEN 1990/1991)

33

Barking Rail Handling Services
Distribution Depot - Isis Link
RL
Car Terminal
C & W Dagenham Storage
Ford Works
Freight Depot
Ripple Lane Yard
Ripple Lane FLT
Dagenham Dock
(DAGENHAM INSET FROM BELOW)
(1:90,000)
Dagenham- Ford Works

B

ESSEX

North Weald
Ongar
C
Epping
Theydon Bois
C
Debden
C
PO Terminal
Chelmsford
Ingatestone
C.S.
Mountnessing Junc.
Shenfield
Billericay
Ingrave Summit
Brentwood

Potters Bar
High Barnet
Cockfosters
P
Enfield Town
Brimsdown
Southbury
Chingford
Mill Hill East
N
(See Map 23)
Hendon Central
N
(See Map 21)
Woodford
C
Hainault
C
(See Map 24)

GREATER LONDON

Chadwell Heath
CE Sdgs.
Romford
Railstore Dist. Dep.
Harold Wood
C.S.
West Horndon
Laindon
Basildon
Gidea Park
LUL Depot
Seven Kings
Ilford
Goodmayes
OLE Depot
Emerson Pk.
D
Upminster
14 13 12 D 10 9 8
2
3
M/D
1
B
C
Barking
North Woolwich
DL
7
6
Dagenham Dock
(SEE INSET ABOVE)
Rainham
Ockendon
Stanford-le-Hope
Thames Haven Junc.
(SEE INSET P34)
Abbey Wood
Belvedere
Erith
Slade Green
Purfleet
Grays
Tilbury Town
East Tilbury
Cliffe Brett Marine
C
Plumstead
Bexleyheath
(See Map 22)
Welling
Barnehurst
Crayford
Dartford
Gravesend
Tilbury Riverside
Hoo Junc.
Hoo Junc. Sdgs.
Higham Tun.
4
5
Falconwood
Albany Park
Sidcup
Bexley
Eltham
KENT
Hoo Staff Halt
Higham

1
0   5   10 m.
0   5   10   15 km.
(1:350,000)

2
DL   DOCKLANDS
B   BAKERLOO
C   CENTRAL
C   CIRCLE
D   DISTRICT
J   JUBILEE

M   METROPOLITAN
M(EL) METROPOLITAN (East London)
N   NORTHERN
P   PICCADILLY
V   VICTORIA

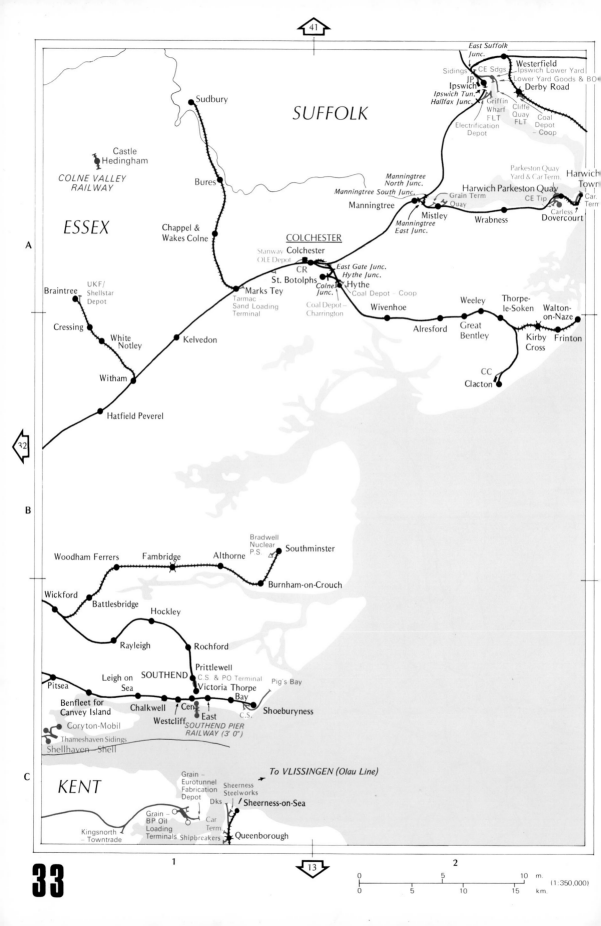

SUFFOLK

East Suffolk
Junc.
Sidings
CE Sdgs
Westerfield
Ipswich Lower Yard
Lower Yard Goods & BO
Ipswich
JP
Derby Road
Ipswich Tun.
Halifax Junc.
Griffin
Wharf
FLT
Cliffe
Quay
FLT
Coal Depot
– Coop
Electrification
Depot

Sudbury

Castle
Hedingham
COLNE VALLEY
RAILWAY

ESSEX

Bures

Chappel &
Wakes Colne

Manningtree
North Junc.
Manningtree South Junc.
Manningtree

Harwich Parkeston Quay
Parkeston Quay
Yard & Car Term.
Harwich
Town
Car.
Term.

Grain Term
Quay
Mistley
Manningtree
East Junc.
Wrabness
CE Tip
Carless
Dovercourt

COLCHESTER
Stanway
OLE Depot
Colchester
CR
St. Botolphs
East Gate Junc.
Hythe Junc.
Colne
Junc.
Hythe
Coal Depot – Coop

A

Marks Tey
Tarmac
Sand Loading
Terminal
Coal Depot –
Charrington

Wivenhoe

Weeley

Thorpe-
le-Soken

Walton-
on-Naze

Braintree
UKF/
Shellstar
Depot

Alresford
Great
Bentley

Kirby
Cross
Frinton

Cressing

White
Notley
Kelvedon

CC
Clacton

Witham

Hatfield Peverel

32

B

Bradwell
Nuclear
P.S.
Southminster

Woodham Ferrers
Fambridge
Althorne

Burnham-on-Crouch

Wickford

Battlesbridge

Hockley

Rayleigh
Rochford

Pitsea

Leigh on
Sea
SOUTHEND
Prittlewell
C.S. & PO Terminal
Pig's Bay

Victoria
Thorpe
Bay
Benfleet for
Canvey Island
Chalkwell
Cen.
East
C.S.
Shoeburyness
Coryton-Mobil
Westcliff
SOUTHEND PIER
RAILWAY (3' 0")
Thameshaven Sidings
Shellhaven – Shell

C

KENT

Grain –
Eurotunnel
Fabrication
Depot
To VLISSINGEN (Olau Line)
Sheerness
Steelworks
Dks
Sheerness-on-Sea

Grain –
BP Oil
Loading
Terminals
Car
Term.
Shipbreakers
Kingsnorth
– Towntrade
Queenborough

1

13

2

0   5   10 m.
0   5   10   15 km.
(1:350,000)

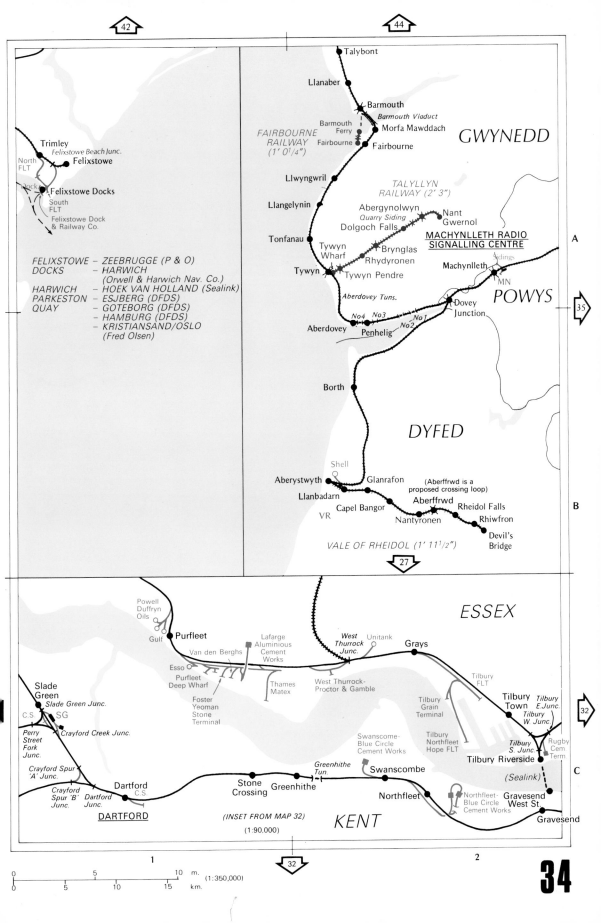

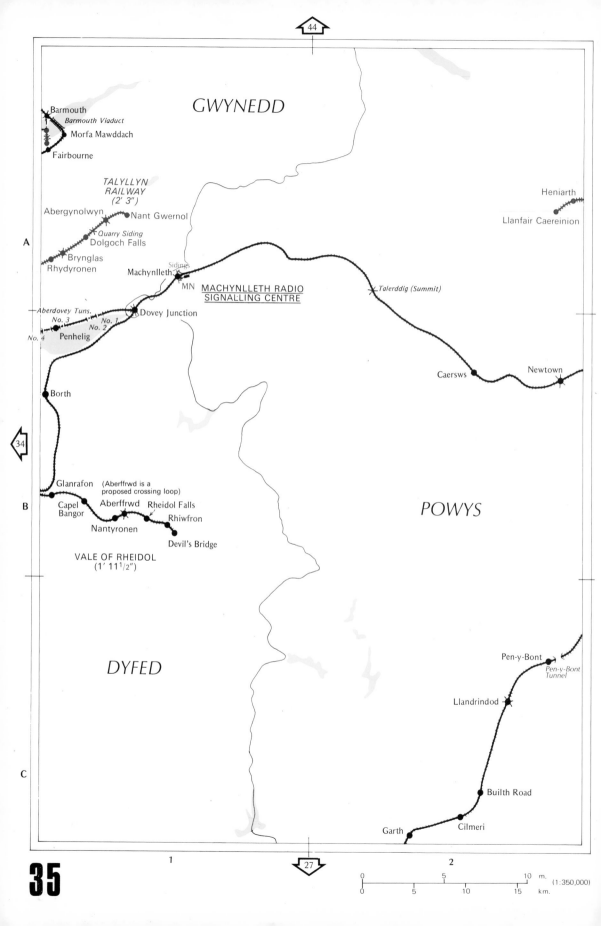

GWYNEDD

Barmouth
Barmouth Viaduct
Morfa Mawddach
Fairbourne

TALYLLYN
RAILWAY
(2' 3")

Abergynolwyn — Nant Gwernol
Quarry Siding
Dolgoch Falls
Brynglas
Rhydyronen

Machynlleth
Sidings

A

MN

MACHYNLLETH RADIO
SIGNALLING CENTRE

Talerddig (Summit)

Aberdovey Tuns.
No. 3   No. 1
          No. 2
No. 4   Penhelig   Dovey Junction

Borth

Caersws   Newtown

34

Glanrafon   (Aberffrwd is a
                    proposed crossing loop)
Capel
Bangor   Aberffrwd   Rheidol Falls
Nantyronen   Rhiwfron
                    Devil's Bridge

POWYS

B

VALE OF RHEIDOL
(1' 11½")

Heniarth
Llanfair Caereinion

DYFED

Pen-y-Bont
*Pen-y-Bont
Tunnel*

Llandrindod

C

Builth Road
Garth   Cilmeri

35

44

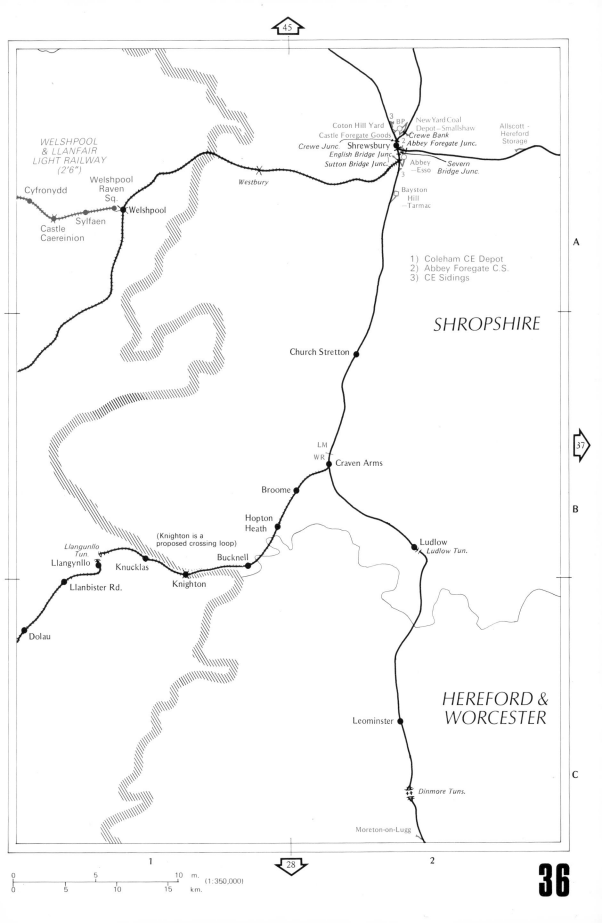

45

WELSHPOOL
& LLANFAIR
LIGHT RAILWAY
(2'6")

Cyfronydd

Welshpool
Raven
Sq.

Sylfaen

Welshpool

Castle
Caereinion

Westbury

Coton Hill Yard
Castle Foregate Goods
Crewe Junc.

New Yard Coal
Depot – Smallshaw
Crewe Bank
Abbey Foregate Junc.

Allscott –
Hereford
Storage

BP
3

Shrewsbury

English Bridge Junc.
Sutton Bridge Junc.

Abbey
–Esso

Severn
Bridge Junc.

3

Bayston
Hill
–Tarmac

A

1) Coleham CE Depot
2) Abbey Foregate C.S.
3) CE Sidings

SHROPSHIRE

Church Stretton

LM
WR
Craven Arms

37

Broome

Hopton
Heath

B

(Knighton is a
proposed crossing loop)

Ludlow
Ludlow Tun.

Llangunllo
Tun.

Llangynllo

Knucklas

Bucknell

Knighton

Llanbister Rd.

Dolau

HEREFORD &
WORCESTER

Leominster

C

Dinmore Tuns.

Moreton-on-Lugg

28

1

2

0   5   10 m.
0   5   10   15 km.

(1:350,000)

36

STAFFORDSHIRE

Colwich Junc.

Shugborough Tun.

Rugeley North Junc.

Rugeley

Brereton Sidings

Rugeley

Lea Hall

Donnington

Wellington
Telford
West

*Stafford
Junc.*
Goods

Penkridge

*Littleton
Coll. Sids.*

Littleton

Hednesford

Rom Ltd
Works

Lichfield
Trent
Valley

*Lichfield
T.V. Junc.*

Oakengates

Tunnel Cement Term.

Oakengates Tun.

Mid Cannock
Opencast

High Level
Goods Loop
Junc.

Lichfield
City

Telford
Central

Shifnal

*Madeley
Junc.*

Cosford

Four Ashes –
Synthetic
Chemicals

Landywood

Brownhills
Charringtons

Ironbridge

Coalbrookdale*

Albrighton

Codsall

Essington
Wood

Bloxwich
North

Brownhills
West

Anglesea
Sidings

CHASEWATER
LIGHT RAILWAY

Shenstone

A

SHROPSHIRE

Bilbrook

Bloxwich

WEST
MIDLANDS

Blake
Street

Butlers
Lane
Four
Oaks

Wolverhampton

Walsall

Bescot

Sutton Coldfield

Wylde Green
Chester Rd.

Erdington
Gravelly
Hill

Bridgnorth

Coseley

Tipton

Dudley Port
Sandwell &
Dudley

Hamstead
Perry Barr

Witton

Aston

Stechford

Lea Ha

Hampton
Loade

*SEVERN
VALLEY
RAILWAY*

Highley

Smethwick
West

Cradley
Heath

Rowley
Regis

Langley
Green

5

3 8

1

4

36

Arley

Stourbridge Town

Lye

Old Hill
(SEE MAP 87)

University

Five
Ways

2

(SEE
MAP 88)

7

6

Tyseley

Acocks
Green

B

Northwood Halt

Kidderminster
Town

Blakedown

Stourbridge
Junction

Hagley

Selly Oak
Bournville

King's Norton

Lifford West Junc.

*Lif.
E. Junc.*

Spring
Road

Yardley
Wood

Hall
Green

Olton

Bewdley

*Foley
Park Tun.*

Kidderminster

Northfield

Car
Term

Whitlock's
End

Solihull

Shirley

Widney
Manor

Longbridge-
Austin Rover

Cofton Hackett
– Austin Rover

Longbridge

*Halesowen
Junc.*

Wythall

Earlswood

The Lakes

Hartlebury

Elmley Lovett –
Anglia Agricultural
Merchants

Barnt Green

LM
WR

*Blackwell
Summit*

Alvechurch

Wood End Tun.

Wood End

Danzey

LM
WR

Hallam Oil

Bromsgrove

*Stoke
Works Junc.*

Redditch

Henley-in-
Arden

Droitwich
Spa

Wootton
Wawen

HEREFORD &
WORCESTER

C

*Rainbow
Hill Tun.*

Worcester
Foregate St.

Henwick

Tunnel Junc.

CE Sidings

Worcester
Shrub Hill

Metal
Box Co.

1) Birmingham New St.
2) Birmingham Moor St.
3) Birmingham Snow Hill
4) Adderley Park
5) Smethwick Rolfe St.
6) Small Heath
7) Bordesley
8) Duddeston

(Henley to
Bearley Junc.
is proposed
for closure)

(still open
late '00)
no ref to thread

Malvern Link

*Norton
Junc.*

*Abbotswood
Junc.*

Pershore

(Proposed remodelling will
eliminate Norton Junc., with
Pershore and Abbotswood single
lines joining at Shrub Hill)

37

0   5   10 m.

0   5   10   15 km.

(1:350,000)

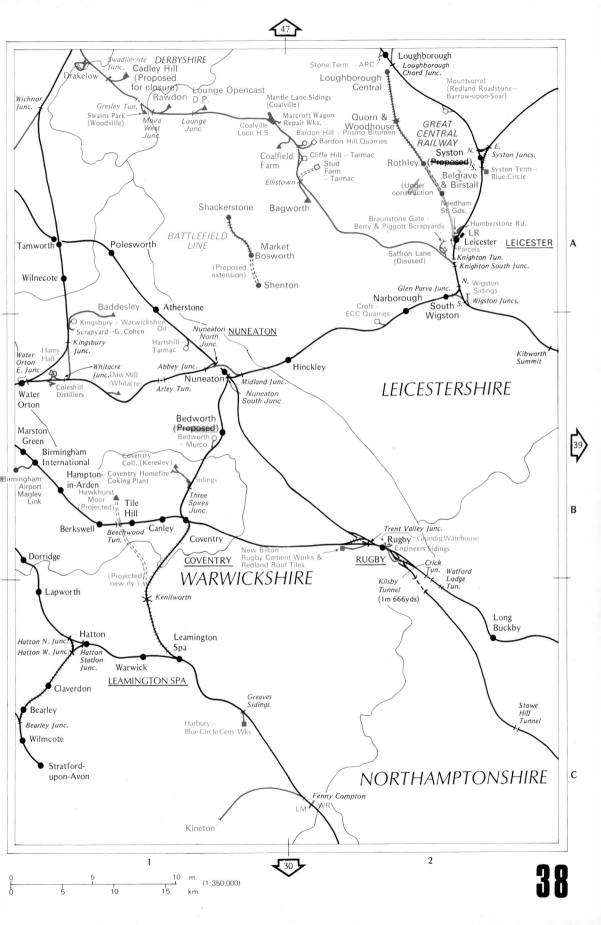

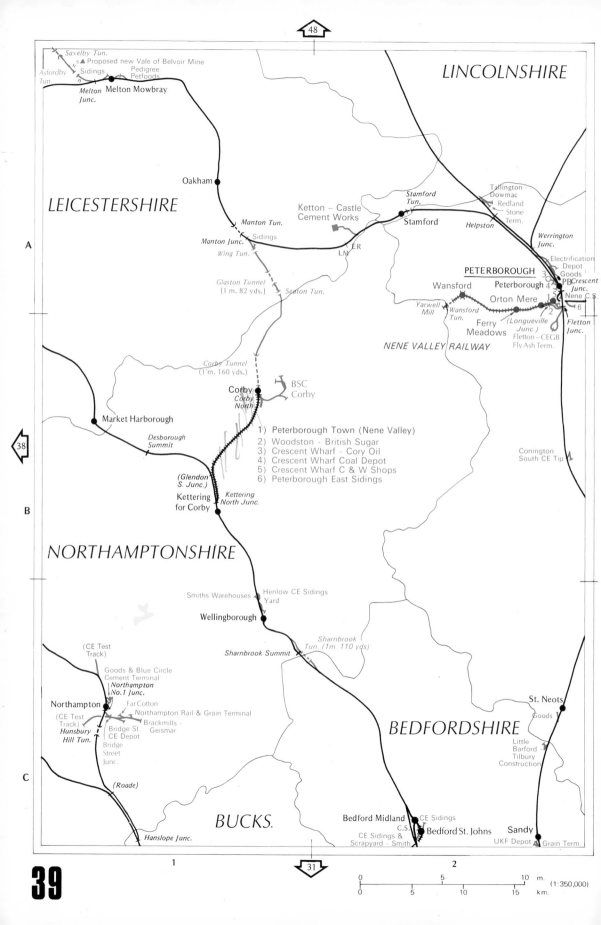

Saxelby Tun.
Astordby Tun. Sidings
Melton Junc. Melton Mowbray
▲ Proposed new Vale of Belvoir Mine
Pedigree Petfoods

LINCOLNSHIRE

LEICESTERSHIRE

Oakham

Ketton – Castle Cement Works

Stamford Tun.
Stamford

Tallington
Dowmac
Redland
Stone Term.

Helpston

Werrington Junc.

PETERBOROUGH

Electrification
Depot
Goods

Wansford

Peterborough

3
Crescent
4 Junc.
PB
Nene C.S.

Orton Mere

Yarwell Mill
Wansford Tun.

1
2
6
Fletton Junc.

A

Manton Tun.
Sidings
Manton Junc.
Wing Tun.
ER
LM

Glaston Tunnel
(1 m. 82 yds.)
Seaton Tun.

Ferry Meadows

(Longueville Junc.)
Fletton – CEGB
Fly Ash Term.

NENE VALLEY RAILWAY

Corby Tunnel
(1 m. 160 yds.)

Corby
Corby North

BSC Corby

Market Harborough

Desborough Summit

38

1) Peterborough Town (Nene Valley)
2) Woodston - British Sugar
3) Crescent Wharf - Cory Oil
4) Crescent Wharf Coal Depot
5) Crescent Wharf C & W Shops
6) Peterborough East Sidings

Conington South CE Tip

B

(Glendon S. Junc.)
Kettering for Corby
Kettering North Junc.

NORTHAMPTONSHIRE

Smiths Warehouses
Henlow CE Sidings Yard

Wellingborough

Sharnbrook Tun. (1m. 110 yds)
Sharnbrook Summit

(CE Test Track)
Goods & Blue Circle Cement Terminal
Northampton No.1 Junc.
Northampton
(CE Test Track)
Hunsbury Hill Tun.
Far Cotton
Northampton Rail & Grain Terminal
Brackmills - Geismar
Bridge St. CE Depot
Bridge Street Junc.

St. Neots
Goods

BEDFORDSHIRE

Little
Barford
Tilbury
Construction

C

(Roade)

BUCKS.

Hanslope Junc.

Bedford Midland
CE Sidings
C.S.
CE Sidings & Scrapyard - Smith
Bedford St. Johns

Sandy
UKF Depot
Grain Term.

0   5   10 m.
0   5   10   15 km.
(1:350,000)

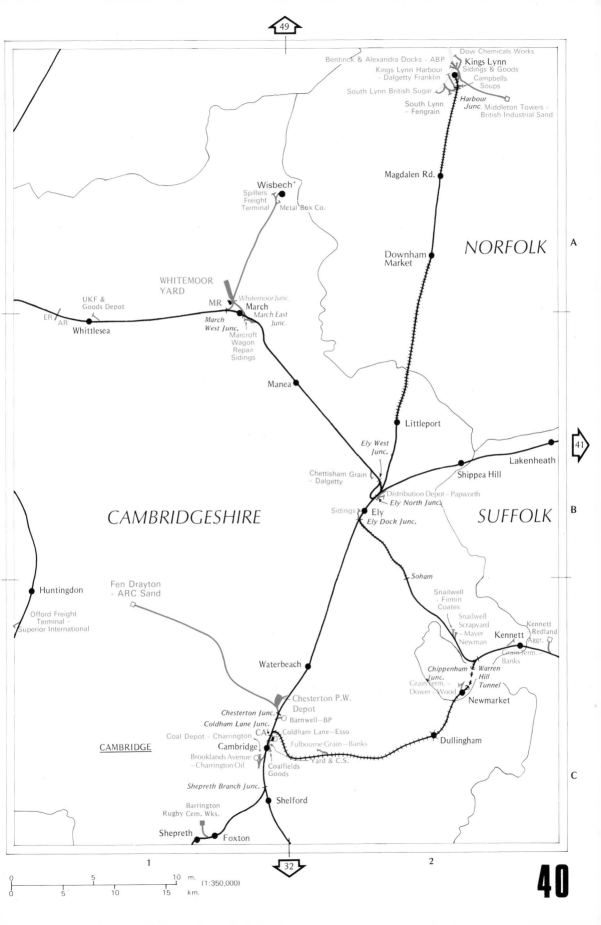

Bentinck & Alexandra Docks - ABP
Dow Chemicals Works
Kings Lynn Harbour - Dalgetty Franklin
Kings Lynn
Sidings & Goods
Campbells Soups
South Lynn British Sugar
South Lynn – Fengrain
Harbour Junc. Middleton Towers - British Industrial Sand

Magdalen Rd.

NORFOLK

A

Wisbech
Spillers Freight Terminal
Metal Box Co.

Downham Market

WHITEMOOR YARD

MR *Whitemoor Junc.*
March *March East Junc.*
March West Junc.
Marcroft Wagon Repair Sidings

UKF & Goods Depot
ER / AR
Whittlesea

Manea

Littleport

41

Ely West Junc.

Lakenheath

Chettisham Grain – Dalgetty

Shippea Hill

Distribution Depot – Papworth
Ely North Junc.
Sidings Ely
Ely Dock Junc.

CAMBRIDGESHIRE

SUFFOLK

B

Soham

Huntingdon

Fen Drayton - ARC Sand

Snailwell - Firmin Coates
Snailwell Scrapyard – Mayer Newman
Kennett
Kennett Redland Aggr.

Offord Freight Terminal - Superior International

Grain Term. Banks
Kennett

Waterbeach

Chippenham Junc. *Warren Hill Tunnel*
Grain Term. – Dower – Wood
Newmarket

Chesterton P.W. Depot
Chesterton Junc.
Coldham Lane Junc.
Coal Depot - Charrington
CA
Coldham Lane – Esso
Barnwell – BP
Fulbourne Grain – Banks
Dullingham

CAMBRIDGE
Cambridge
Brooklands Avenue – Charrington Oil
Yard & C.S.

C

Coalfields Goods

Shepreth Branch Junc.
Shelford

Barrington Rugby Cem. Wks.

Shepreth Foxton

1   2

0 ___ 5 ___ 10 m.   (1:350,000)
0 _ 5 _ 10 _ 15 km.

40

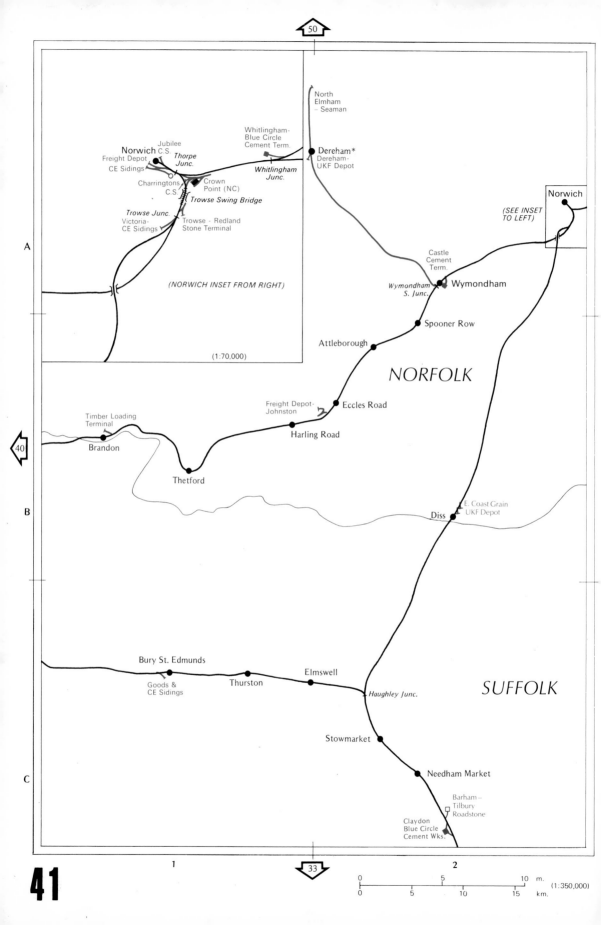

Norwich

(SEE INSET TO LEFT)

(NORWICH INSET FROM RIGHT)

North Elmham – Seaman

Whitlingham- Blue Circle Cement Term.

Jubilee C.S.
Norwich
Freight Depot
CE Sidings
Thorpe Junc.

Charringtons C.S.
Crown Point (NC)

Whitlingham Junc.

Dereham*
Dereham- UKF Depot

Trowse Swing Bridge

Trowse Junc.
Victoria- CE Sidings
Trowse - Redland Stone Terminal

(1:70,000)

Castle Cement Term.

Wymondham S. Junc.
Wymondham

Spooner Row

Attleborough

NORFOLK

Freight Depot- Johnston
Eccles Road

Timber Loading Terminal

Harling Road

Brandon

Thetford

Diss
E. Coast Grain UKF Depot

Bury St. Edmunds
Goods & CE Sidings

Thurston

Elmswell

Haughley Junc.

SUFFOLK

Stowmarket

Needham Market

Barham – Tilbury Roadstone

Claydon Blue Circle Cement Wks.

41

2

0   5   10 m.
0   5   10   15 km.
(1:350,000)

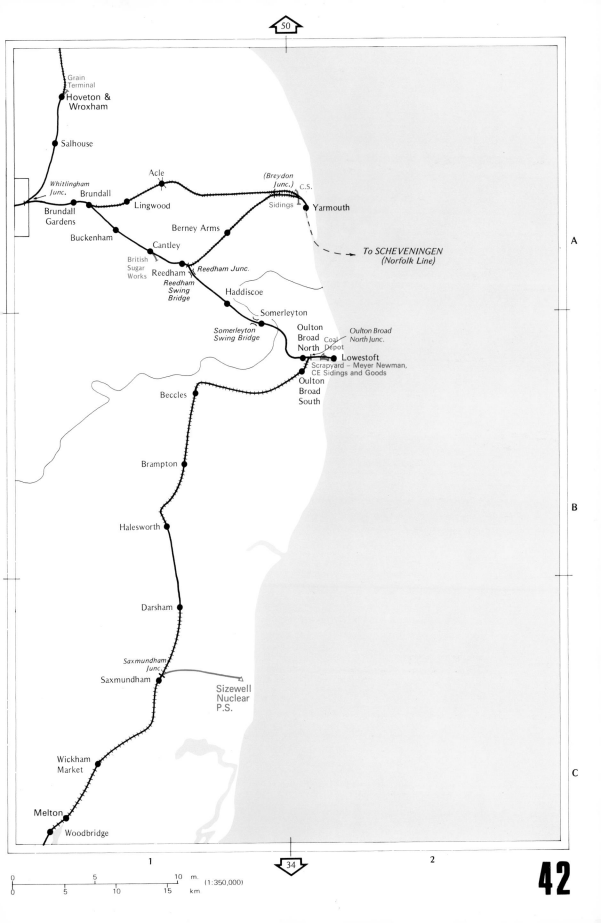

Grain
Terminal
**Hoveton &
Wroxham**

Salhouse

Acle

*Whitlingham
Junc.* Brundall
**Brundall
Gardens** Lingwood

Buckenham

Cantley

*British
Sugar
Works*
Reedham *Reedham Junc.*
*Reedham
Swing
Bridge*

Berney Arms

(*Breydon
Junc.*) C.S.
Sidings Yarmouth

*To SCHEVENINGEN
(Norfolk Line)*

Haddiscoe

Somerleyton

*Somerleyton
Swing Bridge*

Oulton
Broad
North Coal
Depot
*Oulton Broad
North Junc.*
Lowestoft
Scrapyard – Meyer Newman,
CE Sidings and Goods
Oulton
Broad
South

Beccles

Brampton

Halesworth

Darsham

*Saxmundham
Junc.*
Saxmundham
Sizewell
Nuclear
P.S.

Wickham
Market

Melton
Woodbridge

50

34

1   2

A

B

C

0 ___ 5 ___ 10 m.   (1:350,000)
0 _ 5 _ 10 _ 15 km.

42

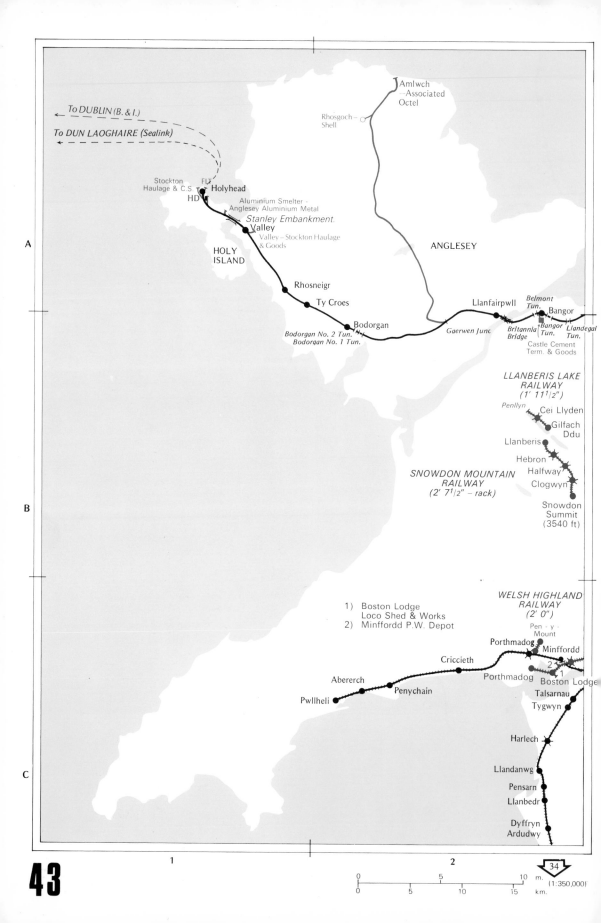

To DUBLIN (B. & I.)

To DUN LAOGHAIRE (Sealink)

Amlwch
—Associated
Octel

Rhosgoch
—Shell

Stockton
Haulage & C.S.
FL
Holyhead
HD
Aluminium Smelter -
Anglesey Aluminium Metal
Stanley Embankment.
Valley
Valley – Stockton Haulage
& Goods

ANGLESEY

HOLY
ISLAND

Rhosneigr

Ty Croes

Llanfairpwll
*Belmont
Tun.*
Bangor

Bodorgan

Bodorgan No. 2 Tun.
Bodorgan No. 1 Tun.

Gaerwen Junc.

*Britannia
Bridge*
*Bangor
Tun.*
*Llandegai
Tun.*

Castle Cement
Term. & Goods

LLANBERIS LAKE
RAILWAY
(1' 11¹/₂")

Penllyn
Cei Llyden
Gilfach
Ddu

Llanberis

Hebron

SNOWDON MOUNTAIN
RAILWAY
(2' 7¹/₂" – rack)

Halfway

Clogwyn

Snowdon
Summit
(3540 ft)

WELSH HIGHLAND
RAILWAY
(2' 0")

1) Boston Lodge
    Loco Shed & Works
2) Minffordd P.W. Depot

Pen - y -
Mount
Porthmadog
Minffordd

Criccieth

2 1
Porthmadog
Boston Lodge

Abererch

Penychain

Talsarnau

Pwllheli

Tygwyn

Harlech

Llandanwg

Pensarn

Llanbedr

Dyffryn
Ardudwy

A

B

C

43

1

2

0   5   10   m.
0   5   10   15   km.

34
(1:350,000)

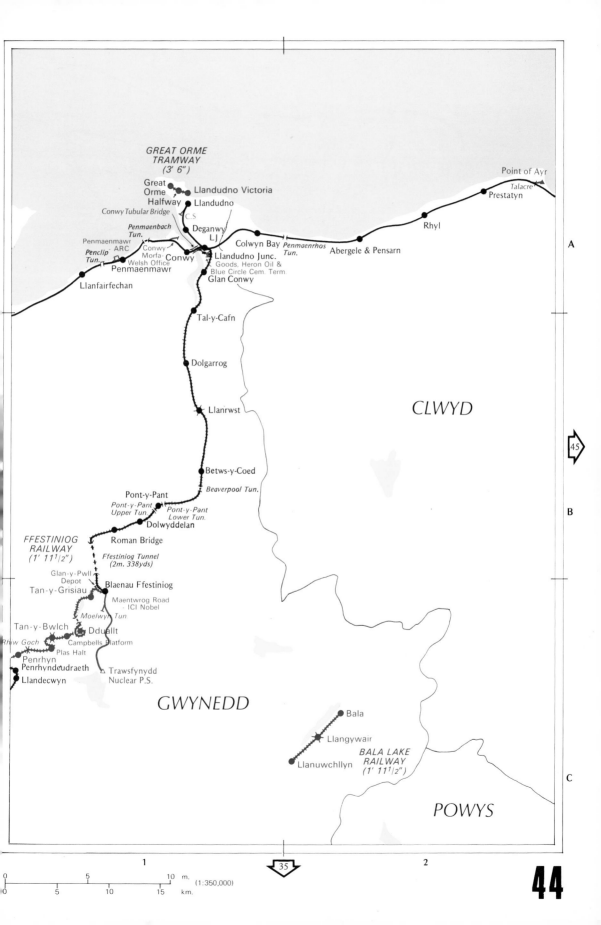

GREAT ORME
TRAMWAY
(3' 6")

Great
Orme
Halfway
Llandudno Victoria
Llandudno

Conwy Tubular Bridge
C.S
Penmaenbach
Tun.
Deganwy
LJ
Point of Ayr
Talacre
Prestatyn

Penmaenmawr
Penclip ARC
Tun.
Conwy
Morfa
Welsh Office
Penmaenmawr
Colwyn Bay
Penmaenrhos
Tun.
Abergele & Pensarn
Rhyl

A

Llanfairfechan
Glan Conwy
Goods, Heron Oil &
Blue Circle Cem. Term.
Llandudno Junc.

Tal-y-Cafn

Dolgarrog

CLWYD

Llanrwst

45

Betws-y-Coed

Pont-y-Pant
Beaverpool Tun.

B

Pont-y-Pant
Upper Tun.
Pont-y-Pant
Lower Tun.
Dolwyddelan

FFESTINIOG
RAILWAY
(1' 11½")
Roman Bridge

Ffestiniog Tunnel
(2m. 338yds)

Glan-y-Pwll
Depot
Tan-y-Grisiau
Blaenau Ffestiniog

Maentwrog Road
- ICI Nobel

Moelwyn Tun.
Tan-y-Bwlch
Dduallt
Rhiw Goch
Campbells Platform
Plas Halt
Penrhyn
Penrhyndeudraeth
Llandecwyn
△ Trawsfynydd
Nuclear P.S.

GWYNEDD

Bala

Llangywair

BALA LAKE
RAILWAY
(1' 11½")
Llanuwchllyn

C

POWYS

1
2

35

0   5   10 m.
(1:350,000)
0   5   10   15 km.

44

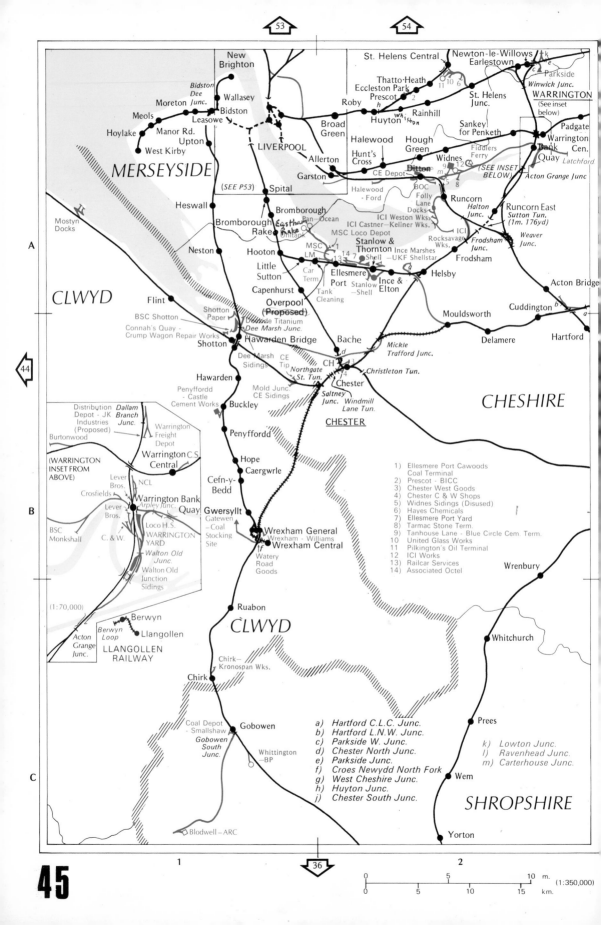

New Brighton

St. Helens Central
Newton-le-Willows
Earlestown

Bidston Dee Junc.
Wallasey
Bidston

Thatto·Heath
Eccleston Park
Prescot
Rainhill

Parkside
c
e
k

Winwick Junc.

WARRINGTON
(See inset below)

Moreton
Leasowe

Roby

St. Helens Junc.

Meols

Broad Green

Huyton
WH
ST DA
h

Sankey for Penketh

Padgate

Hoylake
Manor Rd.
Upton

Halewood

Hough Green

Fiddlers Ferry

Warrington Bank Quay

West Kirby

Hunt's Cross

Widnes

Latchford

MERSEYSIDE

Allerton
Garston

CE Depot
Ditton

(SEE INSET BELOW)

Acton Grange Junc

(SEE P53)
Spital

BOC
Folly Lane Docks

Runcorn

Halton Junc.

Runcorn East
Sutton Tun.
(1m. 176yd)

Heswall

Bromborough
Bromborough Rake

Pan-Ocean
Unilant

Halewood-Ford

ICI Weston Wks.
ICI Castner—Kellner Wks.

Stanlow & Thornton
Ince Marshes

—UKF Shellstar

Weaver Junc.

MSC Loco Depot

Rocksavage Wks.
ICI
Frodsham Junc.

Neston

Hooton

MSC
LM

Ellesmere Port
Stanlow—Shell

Ince & Elton

Helsby

Frodsham

Acton Bridge

Little Sutton

Car Term.

Capenhurst

Tank Cleaning

Mouldsworth

Delamere

Cuddington
b
a

Hartford

Flint

Shotton Paper
Dee Marsh Junc.
Deeside Titanium

Overpool (Proposed)

Bache

CHESHIRE

BSC Shotton
Connah's Quay -
Crump Wagon Repair Works
Shotton

Hawarden Bridge

CH
Mickle Trafford Junc.

Dee Marsh Sidings
CE Tip
Northgate St. Tun.

Christleton Tun.

Hawarden

Mold Junc.
CE Sidings

Saltney Junc.
Windmill Lane Tun.

Chester

CHESTER

Buckley

Penyffordd

Hope

Caergwrle

Cefn-y-Bedd

Gwersyllt

Wrexham General
Wrexham - Williams
Wrexham Central

Watery Road Goods

Wrenbury

1) Ellesmere Port Cawoods
   Coal Terminal
2) Prescot - BICC
3) Chester West Goods
4) Chester C & W Shops
5) Widnes Sidings (Disused)
6) Hayes Chemicals
7) Ellesmere Port Yard
8) Tarmac Stone Term.
9) Tanhouse Lane - Blue Circle Cem. Term.
10) United Glass Works
11) Pilkington's Oil Terminal
12) ICI Works
13) Railcar Services
14) Associated Octel

WARRINGTON INSET

Distribution Depot - JK Industries (Proposed)
Dallam Branch Junc.
Burtonwood
Warrington Freight Depot

(WARRINGTON INSET FROM ABOVE)

Warrington C.S. Central

Lever Bros.
NCL
Crosfields

Lever Bros.

Warrington Bank Quay
Arpley Junc.

BSC Monkshall

C. & W.

Loco H.S.
WARRINGTON YARD

Walton Old Junc.

Walton Old Junction Sidings

(1:70,000)

Berwyn
Berwyn Loop
Llangollen

Ruabon

CLWYD

Acton Grange Junc.

LLANGOLLEN RAILWAY

Whitchurch

Chirk—
Kronospan Wks.

Chirk

Prees

Coal Depot - Smallshaw
Gobowen South Junc.
Gobowen

Whittington—BP

a) Hartford C.L.C. Junc.
b) Hartford L.N.W. Junc.
c) Parkside W. Junc.
d) Chester North Junc.
e) Parkside Junc.
f) Croes Newydd North Fork
g) West Cheshire Junc.
h) Huyton Junc.
j) Chester South Junc.

k) Lowton Junc.
l) Ravenhead Junc.
m) Carterhouse Junc.

Wem

Blodwell - ARC

SHROPSHIRE

Yorton

CLWYD

Mostyn Docks

Penyffordd - Castle Cement Works

1
2
36

0   5   10   m.
0   5   10   15   km.
(1:350,000)

44

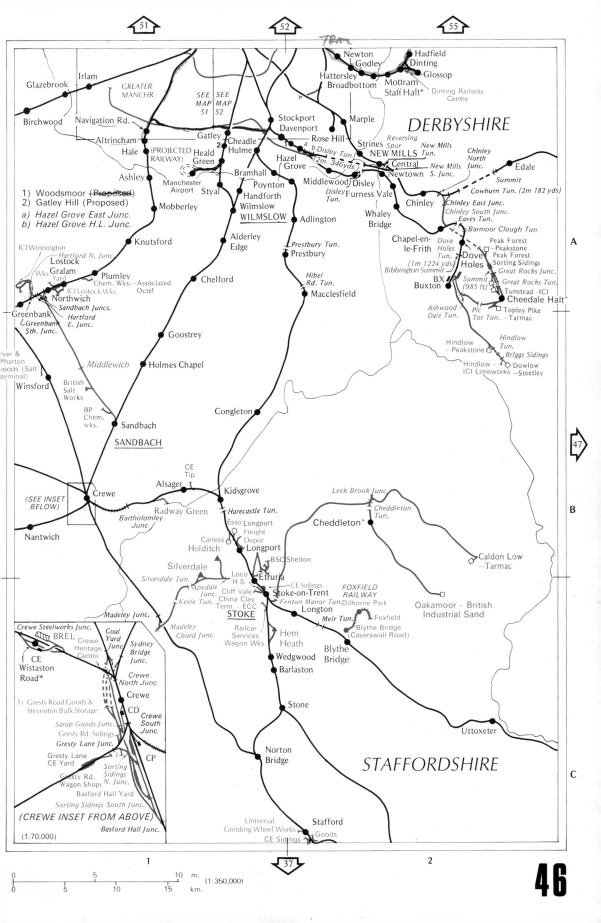

Glazebrook
Irlam
Birchwood

GREATER MANCHR.

SEE MAP 51   SEE MAP 52

Newton
Godley
Hattersley
Broadbottom
Mottram Staff Halt*
Hadfield
Dinting
Glossop
Dinting Railway Centre

DERBYSHIRE

Stockport
Davenport
Marple

Navigation Rd.
Altrincham
Gatley
Cheadle Hulme
Rose Hill
Strines
Reversing Spur
New Mills Tun.

Hale
(PROJECTED RAILWAY)
Heald Green
Hazel Grove
Disley Tun. (2m. 346yds)
a
b
NEW MILLS
Central
Newtown
New Mills
S. Junc.
Chinley North Junc.
Edale

Ashley
Manchester Airport
Bramhall
Poynton
Middlewood
Disley
Furness Vale
Summit
Cowburn Tun. (2m 182 yds)

1) Woodsmoor (Proposed)
2) Gatley Hill (Proposed)
a) Hazel Grove East Junc.
b) Hazel Grove H.L. Junc.

Mobberley
Styal
Handforth
Wilmslow
WILMSLOW
Adlington
Whaley Bridge
Chinley
Chinley East Junc.
Chinley South Junc.
Eaves Tun.
Barmoor Clough Tun.

ICI Winnington
Hartford N. Junc.
Knutsford
Alderley Edge
Prestbury Tun.
Prestbury
Chapel-en-le-Frith
Dove Holes Tun. (1m 1224 yds)
Bibbington Summit
BX
Buxton
Peak Forest
Peakstone
Peak Forest Sorting Sidings
Great Rocks Junc.
Great Rocks Tun.
Tunstead - ICI
Cheedale Halt*

Lostock Gralam
Wks Yard
Plumley
Chem. Wks. – Associated Octel
Chelford
Macclesfield
Hibel Rd. Tun.
Dove Holes
Summit (985 ft)
Topley Pike
Pic Tor Tun. – Tarmac

ICI Lostock Wks.
Northwich
Sandbach Juncs.
Hartford E. Junc.
Goostrey
Ashwood Dale Tun.

Greenbank
Greenbank Sth. Junc.
Hindlow - Peakstone
Hindlow Tun.
Briggs Sidings
Hindlow - ICI Limeworks
Dowlow Steetley

iver & harton oods (Salt erminal)
Winsford
Middlewich
Holmes Chapel
British Salt Works

BP Chem. wks.
Sandbach
Congleton
SANDBACH

CE Tip
Crewe
(SEE INSET BELOW)
Alsager
Radway Green
Bartholomley Junc.
Kidsgrove
Leek Brook Junc.
Cheddleton Tun.
Cheddleton*

Nantwich
Harecastle Tun.
Esso Longport
Freight Depot
Caldon Low – Tarmac

Carless
Holditch
Longport
BSC Shelton

Silverdale
Silverdale Tun.
Loco H.S.
Etruria
CE Sidings
Stoke-on-Trent
FOXFIELD RAILWAY
Dilhorne Park
Oakamoor - British Industrial Sand

Apedale Junc.
Keele Tun.
Cliff Vale
China Clay Term. - ECC
STOKE
Fenton Manor Tun.
Longton
Meir Tun.
Foxfield
Blythe Bridge (Caverswall Road)

Madeley Junc.
Madeley Chord Junc.
Railcar Services Wagon Wks.
Hem Heath
Blythe Bridge

Crewe Steelworks Junc.
BREL
Crewe Heritage Centre
Coal Yard Junc.
Sydney Bridge Junc.
Wedgwood
Barlaston

CE Wistaston Road*
Crewe North Junc.
Crewe
Stone

1) Gresty Road Goods & Steventon Bulk Storage
Salop Goods Junc.
Gresty Rd. Sidings
Gresty Lane Junc.
CD
Crewe South Junc.
CP
Norton Bridge

Gresty Lane CE Yard
Gresty Rd. Wagon Shops
Sorting Sidings N. Junc.
Basford Hall Yard
Sorting Sidings South Junc.
STAFFORDSHIRE

(CREWE INSET FROM ABOVE)
(1:70,000)
Basford Hall Junc.
Universal Grinding Wheel Works
CE Sidings
Stafford
Goods

Uttoxeter

0   5   10 m.
(1:350,000)
0   5   10   15 km.

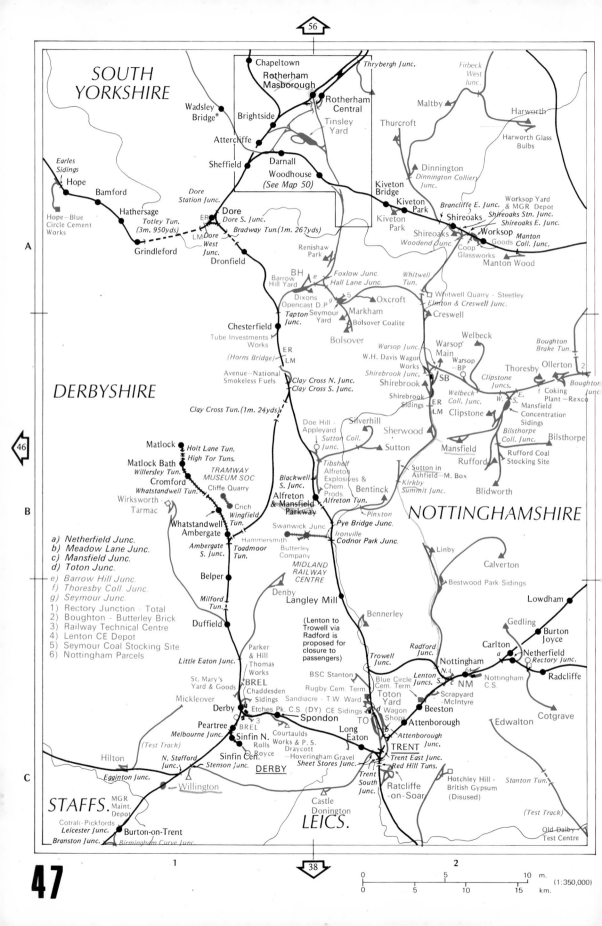

SOUTH
YORKSHIRE

*Earles
Sidings*
Hope

Bamford

Hathersage

Hope–Blue
Circle Cement
Works

Grindleford

Wadsley
Bridge*

Brightside

Attercliffe

Sheffield

*Dore
Station Junc.*

Dore

ER

LM *Dore
West
Junc.*

Dronfield

*Totley Tun.
(3m. 950yds)*

Dore S. Junc.

Bradway Tun.(1m. 267yds)

Chapeltown

Rotherham
Masborough

Rotherham
Central

Darnall

Woodhouse
(See Map 50)

*Tinsley
Yard*

Thrybergh Junc.

*Firbeck
West
Junc.*

Maltby

Harworth

Thurcroft

Harworth Glass
Bulbs

Dinnington
*Dinnington Colliery
Junc.*

Kiveton
Bridge

Kiveton
Park

Kiveton
Park

Shireoaks

Brancliffe E. Junc.

Shireoaks Stn. Junc.
Shireoaks E. Junc.

Worksop Yard
& MGR Depot

Worksop

*Manton
Coll. Junc.*

Goods

Manton Wood

Woodend Junc.

Coop
Glassworks

*Renishaw
Park*

BH

BARROW
HILL YARD

*Barrow
Hill Yard*

e

g

*Foxlow Junc.
Hall Lane Junc.*

Dixons
Opencast D.P.

*Tapton
Junc.*

Seymour
Yard

5

Markham

Bolsover Coalite

Oxcroft

Creswell

*Whitwell
Tun.*

Whitwell Quarry - Steetley
Elmton & Creswell Junc.

Welbeck

*Boughton
Brake Tun.*

Chesterfield

*Tube Investments
Works*

ER
LM

(Horns Bridge)

Bolsover

Warsop
Main

Warsop Junc.

W.H. Davis Wagon
Works

Shirebrook Junc.

Shirebrook

Warsop
-BP

SB

Thoresby

Ollerton

2

*Clipstone
Juncs.*

*Boughton
Junc.*

Coking
Plant - Rexco

E.

W.S.

Mansfield
Concentration
Sidings

Bilsthorpe

*Avenue–National
Smokeless Fuels*

*Clay Cross N. Junc.
Clay Cross S. Junc.*

*Shirebrook
Sidings*

ER
LM

*Welbeck
Coll. Junc.*

Clipstone

*Bilsthorpe
Coll. Junc.*

DERBYSHIRE

Clay Cross Tun. (1m. 24yds)

Doe Hill -
Appleyard

*Sutton Coll.
Junc.*

Silverhill

Sherwood

Sutton

Mansfield

Rufford

*Rufford Coal
Stocking Site*

Matlock

Holt Lane Tun.
High Tor Tuns.

Matlock Bath

Willersley Tun.

Cromford

Whatstandwell Tun.

Wirksworth
Tarmac

TRAMWAY
MUSEUM SOC

Cliffe Quarry

Crich

*Wingfield
Tun.*

Whatstandwell

Ambergate

*Blackwell
S. Junc.*

Alfreton
& Mansfield
Parkway

*Tibshelf
Alfreton
Explosives &
Chem.
Prods*

Alfreton Tun.

Bentinck

Sutton in
Ashfield–M. Box

*Kirkby
Summit Junc.*

Blidworth

NOTTINGHAMSHIRE

a) *Netherfield Junc.*
b) *Meadow Lane Junc.*
c) *Mansfield Junc.*
d) *Toton Junc.*
e) *Barrow Hill Junc.*
f) *Thoresby Coll. Junc.*
g) *Seymour Junc.*
1) Rectory Junction - Total
2) Boughton - Butterley Brick
3) Railway Technical Centre
4) Lenton CE Depot
5) Seymour Coal Stocking Site
6) Nottingham Parcels

*Ambergate
S. Junc.*

Belper

*Toadmoor
Tun.*

Swanwick Junc.

Hammersmith

Butterley
Company

MIDLAND
RAILWAY
CENTRE

Denby

Pinxton

Pye Bridge Junc.

Ironville
Codnor Park Junc.

Linby

Calverton

Langley Mill

Bennerley

Bestwood Park Sidings

Lowdham

*Milford
Tun.*

Duffield

Parker
& Hill
Thomas
Works

(Lenton to
Trowell via
Radford is
proposed for
closure to
passengers)

*Radford
Junc.*

*Trowell
Junc.*

Gedling

Burton
Joyce

Carlton

a

Netherfield

Rectory Junc.

Radcliffe

Little Eaton Junc.

St. Mary's
Yard & Goods

Mickleover

Derby

BREL

*Chaddesden
Sidings*

Etches Pk. C.S. (DY)

Spondon

BSC Stanton

Rugby Cem. Term.

Sandiacre - T.W. Ward

CE Sidings

Blue Circle
Cem. Term.

*Lenton
Juncs.*

c

N.4.

S.

NM

Nottingham
C.S.

Cotgrave

Peartree

Melbourne Junc.

Sinfin N.

Sinfin Cen.

BREL

Courtaulds
Works & P.S.
Draycott

Rolls
Royce

Long
Eaton

Toton
Yard

TO

Scrapyard
-McIntyre

d Wagon
Shops

Beeston

Attenborough

*Attenborough
Junc.*

Edwalton

Hilton

*N. Stafford
Junc.*

Stenson Junc.

(Test Track)

Egginton Junc.

DERBY

Willington

Hoveringham Gravel

Sheet Stores Junc.

Trent East Junc.
Red Hill Tuns.

TRENT

*Trent South
Junc.*

Ratcliffe
-on-Soar

Hotchley Hill -
British Gypsum
(Disused)

Stanton Tun.

STAFFS.

MGR
Maint.
Depot

Cotrali-Pickfords
Leicester Junc.

Burton-on-Trent

Branston Junc.

Birmingham Curve Junc.

Castle
Donington

LEICS.

(Test Track)

Old Dalby
Test Centre

1

2

0   5   10 m.

0   5   10   15   km.

(1:350,000)

46

A

B

C

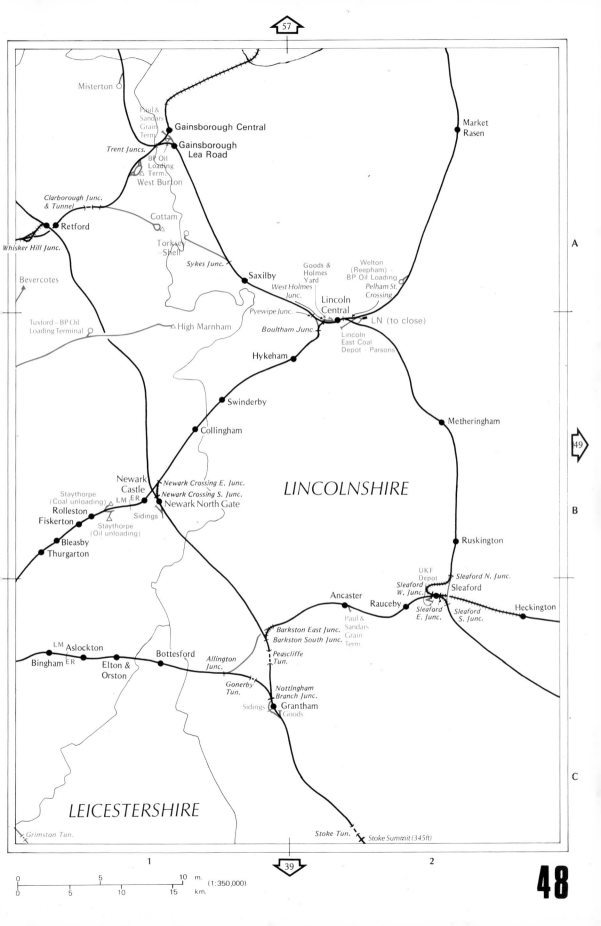

Misterton

Paul & Sandars Grain Term.

Gainsborough Central

Gainsborough Lea Road

Trent Juncs.

BP Oil Loading Term.

West Burton

Market Rasen

Clarborough Junc. & Tunnel

Cottam

Retford

Whisker Hill Junc.

Torksey Shell

A

Bevercotes

Sykes Junc.

Saxilby

Goods & Holmes Yard

West Holmes Junc.

Welton (Reepham) BP Oil Loading

Pelham St. Crossing

Tuxford – BP Oil Loading Terminal

△ High Marnham

Pyewipe Junc.

Lincoln Central

LN (to close)

Boultham Junc.

Lincoln East Coal Depot - Parsons

Hykeham

Swinderby

Metheringham

Collingham

49

Newark Castle

Newark Crossing E. Junc.

Newark Crossing S. Junc.

LM ER

Newark North Gate

LINCOLNSHIRE

Staythorpe (Coal unloading)

Rolleston

Fiskerton

Sidings

Staythorpe (Oil unloading)

B

Bleasby

Thurgarton

Ruskington

UKF Depot

Sleaford N. Junc.

Sleaford W. Junc.

Sleaford

Ancaster

Rauceby

Sleaford E. Junc.

Sleaford S. Junc.

Heckington

Paul & Sandars Grain Term.

Barkston East Junc.

Barkston South Junc.

LM Aslockton

Bingham ER

Elton & Orston

Bottesford

Allington Junc.

Peascliffe Tun.

Gonerby Tun.

Nottingham Branch Junc.

Sidings

Grantham

Goods

C

LEICESTERSHIRE

✕ *Grimston Tun.*

Stoke Tun.

Stoke Summit (345ft)

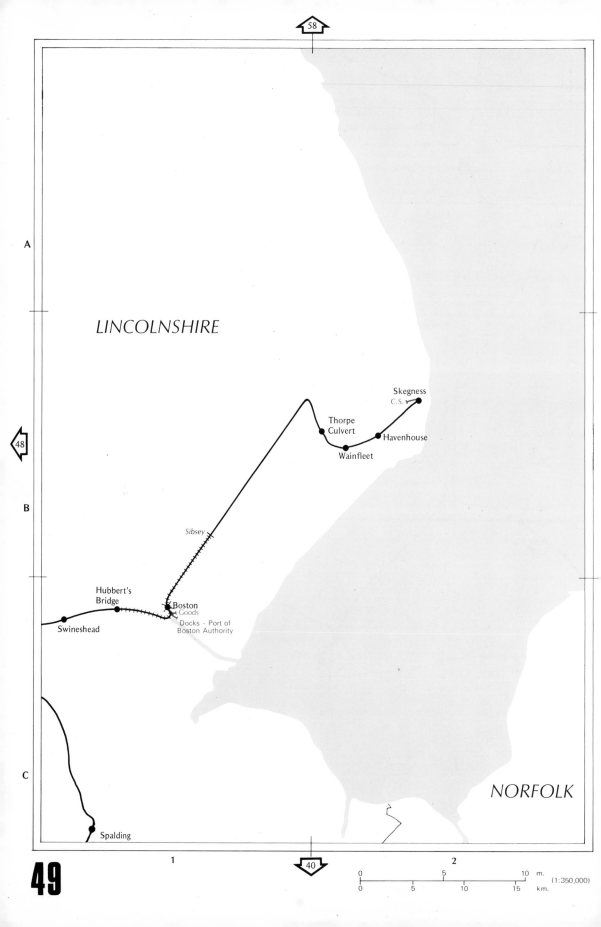

A

LINCOLNSHIRE

Skegness
C.S.

Thorpe
Culvert

48

Havenhouse

Wainfleet

B

Sibsey

Hubbert's
Bridge

Boston
Goods

Swineshead

Docks - Port of
Boston Authority

C

NORFOLK

Spalding

0   5   10 m.
                        (1:350,000)
0   5   10   15
                      km.

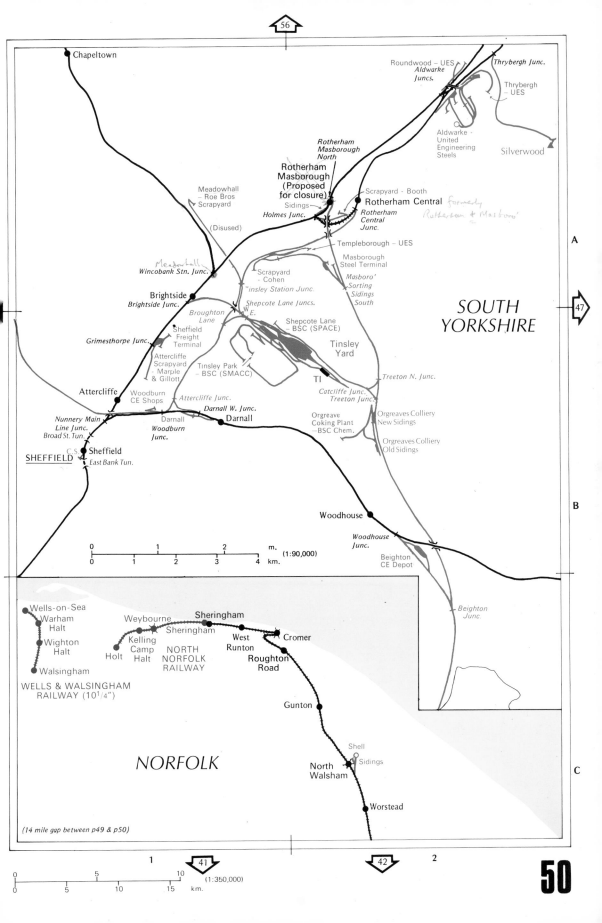

Chapeltown

Roundwood – UES
Aldwarke
Juncs.
Thrybergh Junc.

Thrybergh
– UES

Aldwarke -
United
Engineering
Steels

Silverwood

Rotherham
Masbrough
North

Meadowhall
– Roe Bros
Scrapyard

Rotherham
Masborough
(Proposed
for closure)

Sidings

Scrapyard - Booth

Rotherham Central *formerly*

Rotherham & Masboro'

Holmes Junc.

Rotherham
Central
Junc.

(Disused)

Templeborough – UES

Masborough
Steel Terminal

Meadowhall

Scrapyard
- Cohen

Masboro'
Sorting
Sidings
South

Wincobank Stn. Junc.

Tinsley Station Junc.

Shepcote Lane Juncs.
W. E.

SOUTH
YORKSHIRE

Brightside
Brightside Junc.

Broughton
Lane

Shepcote Lane
– BSC (SPACE)

Grimesthorpe Junc.

Sheffield
Freight
Terminal

Tinsley
Yard

Attercliffe
Scrapyard
- Marple
& Gillott

Tinsley Park
– BSC (SMACC)

TI

Treeton N. Junc.

Attercliffe

Woodburn
CE Shops

Attercliffe Junc.

Catcliffe Junc.
Treeton Junc.

Orgreaves Colliery
New Sidings

Darnall W. Junc.

Orgreave
Coking Plant
–BSC Chem.

Nunnery Main
Line Junc.
Broad St. Tun.

Darnall

Darnall

Woodburn
Junc.

Orgreaves Colliery
Old Sidings

SHEFFIELD

C.S.

Sheffield
East Bank Tun.

Woodhouse

Woodhouse
Junc.

Beighton
CE Depot

0   1   2   m.
──────────────── (1:90,000)
0 1 2 3 4 km.

Wells-on-Sea
Warham Halt

Beighton
Junc.

Wighton
Halt

Weybourne

Sheringham

Sheringham

Kelling
Camp
Halt

West
Runton

Cromer

Walsingham

Holt

NORTH
NORFOLK
RAILWAY

Roughton
Road

WELLS & WALSINGHAM
RAILWAY (10¼")

NORFOLK

Gunton

Shell
Sidings

North
Walsham

Worstead

(14 mile gap between p49 & p50)

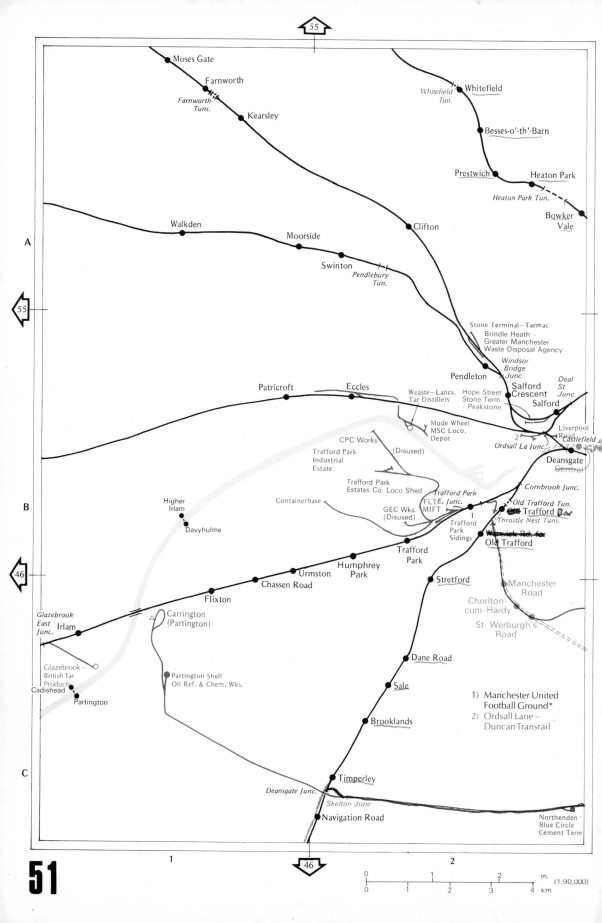

Moses Gate

Farnworth

Farnworth Tuns.

Kearsley

Whitefield Tun.

Whitefield

Besses-o'-th'-Barn

Prestwich

Heaton Park

Heaton Park Tun.

Bowker Vale

Walkden

A

Moorside

Clifton

Swinton

Pendlebury Tun.

Stone Terminal–Tarmac
Brindle Heath –
Greater Manchester
Waste Disposal Agency

Windsor Bridge Junc.

Pendleton

Deal St. Junc.

Patricroft

Eccles

Weaste–Lancs.
Tar Distillers

Hope Street
Stone Term.
- Peakstone

Salford Crescent

Salford

Mode Wheel
MSC Loco.
Depot

Liverpool Road

Castlefield

2

Ordsall La Junc.

CPC Works

(Disused)

Trafford Park
Industrial
Estate

Deansgate

Central

Cornbrook Junc.

Trafford Park
Estates Co. Loco Shed

Trafford Park FLT E. Junc.

MIFT

Old Trafford Tun.

Old Trafford Bar

B

Higher
Irlam

Davyhulme

Containerbase

GEC Wks.
(Disused)

1

Trafford
Park
Sidings

Throstle Nest Tuns.

Warwick Rd. for
Old Trafford

Trafford
Park

Humphrey
Park

Urmston

Chassen Road

Stretford

Manchester
Road

46

Flixton

Glazebrook East Junc.

Irlam

Carrington
(Partington)

Chorlton-
cum-Hardy

St. Werburgh's
Road

Glazebrook –
British Tar
Products

Cadishead

Partington

Partington Shell
Oil Ref. & Chem. Wks.

Dane Road

Sale

1) Manchester United
Football Ground*
2) Ordsall Lane –
Duncan Transrail

Brooklands

C

Timperley

Deansgate Junc.

Skelton Junc.

Navigation Road

Northenden
Blue Circle
Cement Term

1

2

0   1   2   m. (1:90,000)
0   1   2   3   4   km

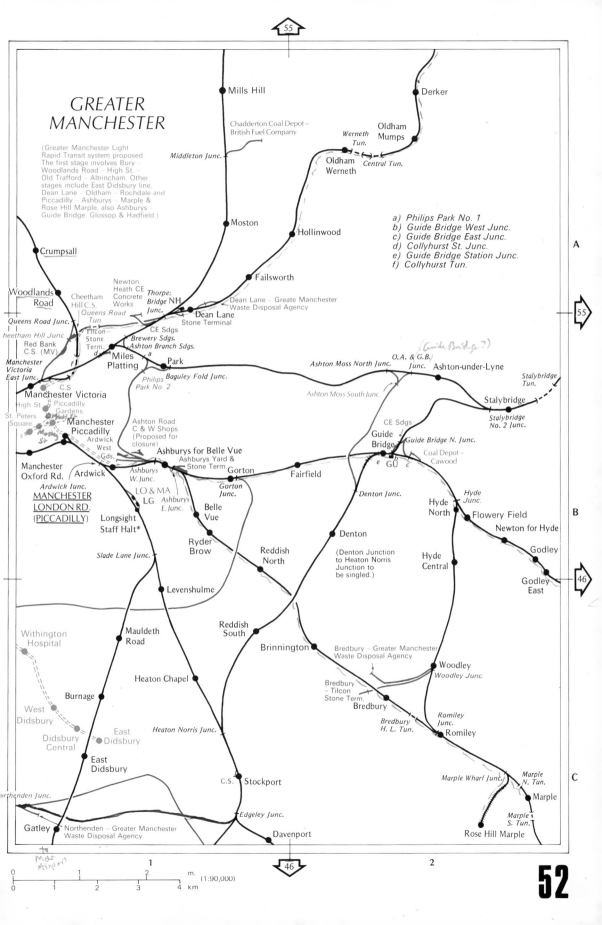

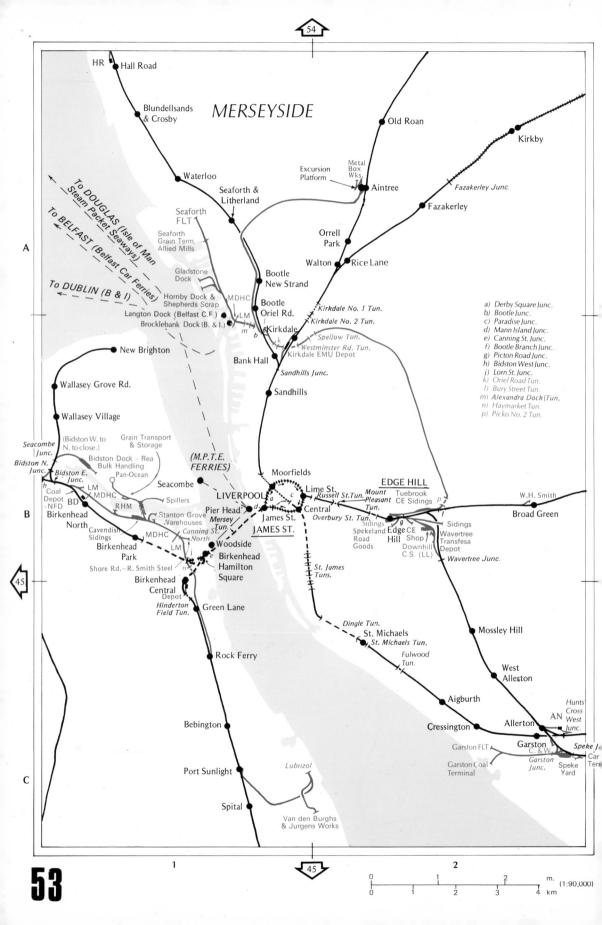

MERSEYSIDE

HR Hall Road

Blundellsands & Crosby

Waterloo

Old Roan

Kirkby

Seaforth & Litherland

Seaforth FLT

Excursion Platform

Metal Box Wks.

Aintree

Fazakerley Junc.

Fazakerley

A

Seaforth Grain Term. Allied Mills

To DOUGLAS (Isle of Man) Steam Packet Seaways

To BELFAST (Belfast Car Ferries)

To DUBLIN (B & I)

Gladstone Dock

Hornby Dock & Shepherds Scrap

Langton Dock (Belfast C.F.)

Brocklebank Dock (B. & I.)

MDHC

LM

Bootle New Strand

Bootle Oriel Rd.

Kirkdale

Orrell Park

Walton

Rice Lane

Kirkdale No. 1 Tun.

Kirkdale No. 2 Tun.

Spellow Tun.

Westminster Rd. Tun.

Kirkdale EMU Depot

a) Derby Square Junc.
b) Bootle Junc.
c) Paradise Junc.
d) Mann Island Junc.
e) Canning St. Junc.
f) Bootle Branch Junc.
g) Picton Road Junc.
h) Bidston West Junc.
j) Lorn St. Junc.
k) Oriel Road Tun.
l) Bury Street Tun.
m) Alexandra Dock Tun.
n) Haymarket Tun.
p) Picko No. 2 Tun.

New Brighton

Wallasey Grove Rd.

Wallasey Village

Bank Hall

Sandhills Junc.

Sandhills

Seacombe Junc.

Bidston N. Junc.

(Bidston W. to N. to close.)

Grain Transport & Storage

Bidston E. Junc.

Bidston Dock – Rea Bulk Handling Pan-Ocean

Seacombe

(M.P.T.E. FERRIES)

Moorfields

LIVERPOOL

Lime St.

EDGE HILL

Tuebrook CE Sidings

W.H. Smith

Broad Green

h

Coal Depot –NFD

BD

LM MDHC

RHM

Spillers

Stanton Grove Warehouses

Canning St. North

Mersey Tun.

Pier Head

James St.

Central

JAMES ST.

Russell St.Tun.

Mount Pleasant Tun.

Overbury St. Tun.

Sidings

Spekeland Road Goods

Edge Hill

CE Shop

Downhill C.S. (LL)

Sidings

Wavertree Transfesa Depot

Wavertree Junc.

Birkenhead North

Cavendish Sidings

Birkenhead Park

MDHC

LM

j

Woodside

e

Birkenhead Hamilton Square

Shore Rd.–R. Smith Steel

n

Birkenhead Central

Depot

Hinderton Field Tun.

Green Lane

St. James Tuns.

Dingle Tun.

St. Michaels

St. Michaels Tun.

Fulwood Tun.

Mossley Hill

West Allerton

Rock Ferry

Aigburth

Cressington

Allerton

Hunts Cross West Junc.

AN

Garston

C. & W.

Speke J Car Ter

Bebington

Garston FLT

Garston Junc.

Garston Coal Terminal

Speke Yard

Port Sunlight

Lubrizol

Spital

Van den Burghs & Jurgens Works

m. (1:90,000)

km

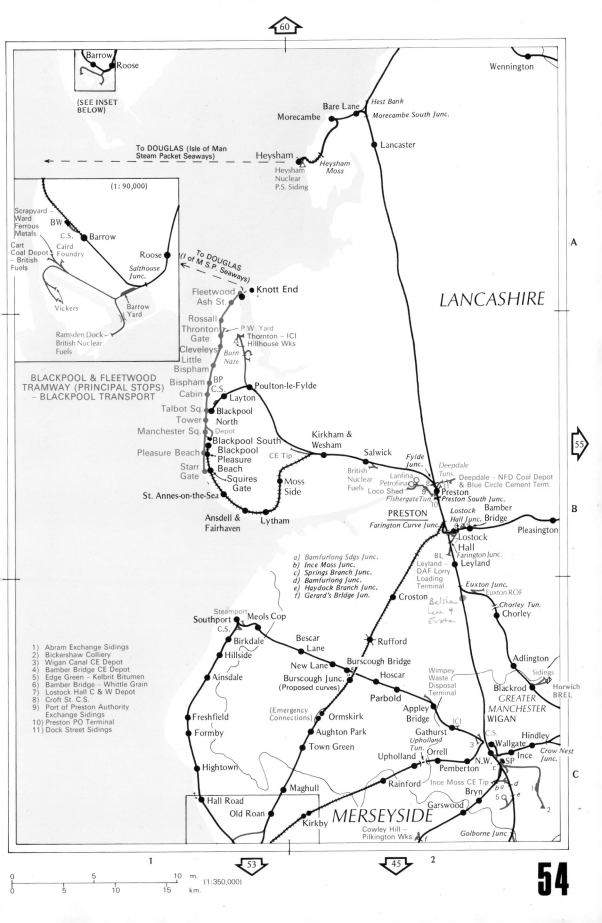

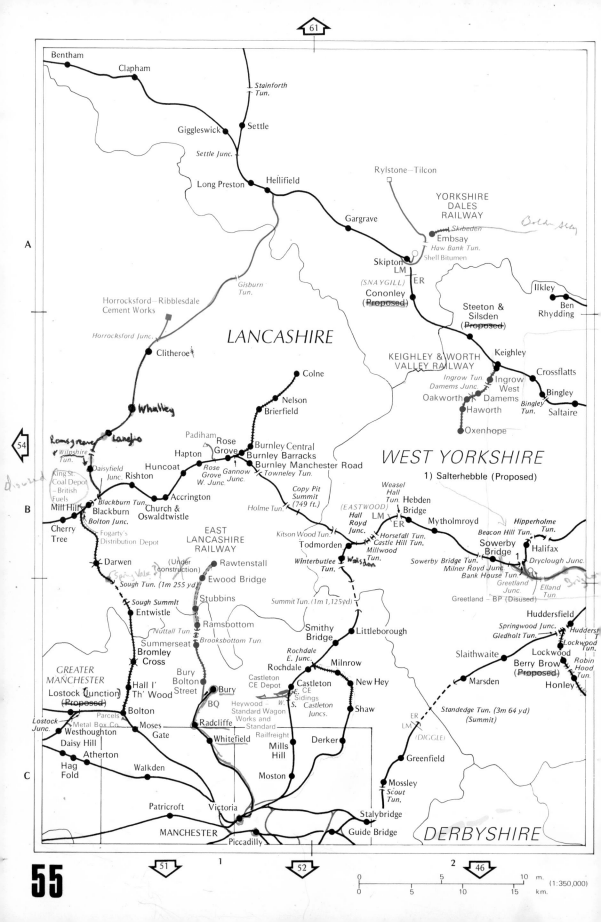

Bentham
Clapham
Stainforth Tun.
Settle
Giggleswick
Settle Junc.
Long Preston
Hellifield
Gargrave
Rylstone – Tilcon
YORKSHIRE
DALES
RAILWAY
Bold seg
Skibeden
Embsay
Haw Bank Tun.
Skipton
LM
(SNAYGILL)
Shell Bitumen
ER
Cononley
(Proposed)
Ilkley
Ben Rhydding
Steeton &
Silsden
(Proposed)

A

Gisburn Tun.
Horrocksford – Ribblesdale
Cement Works

LANCASHIRE

Keighley
Crossflatts
KEIGHLEY & WORTH
VALLEY RAILWAY
Ingrow Tun.
Ingrow
West
Bingley
Damems Junc.
Oakworth
Damems
Bingley Tun.
Saltaire
Horrocksford Junc.
Clitheroe
Haworth
Oxenhope

Colne
Nelson
Brierfield
Whalley
Ramsgrave Langho
WEST YORKSHIRE

1) Salterhebble (Proposed)

Wilpshire Tun.
Daisyfield Junc.
Padiham
Rose Grove
Hapton
Burnley Central
Burnley Barracks
Burnley Manchester Road
Rose Grove W. Junc.
Gannow Junc.
Towneley Tun.
Weasel Hall Tun.
Hebden Bridge
Mytholmroyd
Hipperholme Tun.

54

Huncoat
Rishton
Copy Pit Summit (749 ft.)
(EASTWOOD)
Hall Royd Junc.
LM
ER
Beacon Hill Tun.
Sowerby Bridge
Halifax
discard

B

King St.
Coal Depot
– British
Fuels
Blackburn Tun.
Accrington
Church &
Oswaldtwistle
Holme Tun.
Kitson Wood Tun.
Horsefall Tun.
Castle Hill Tun.
Millwood
Tun.
Todmorden
Sowerby Bridge Tun.
1
Dryclough Junc.
Mill Hill
Blackburn
Bolton Junc.
EAST
LANCASHIRE
RAILWAY
Winterbutlee Tun.
Walsden
Milner Royd Junc.
Bank House Tun.
Greetland Junc.
Elland Tun.
Bridge
Cherry
Tree
Fogarty's Distribution Depot
Greetland – BP (Disused)

Darwen
(Spring Vale ?)
(Under construction)
Rawtenstall
Ewood Bridge
Summit Tun. (1m 1,125 yd)
Huddersfield
Springwood Junc.
Gledholt Tun.
Huddersfield
Lockwood Tun.
Sough Tun. (1m 255 yd)
Stubbins
Littleborough
Slaithwaite
Lockwood
Berry Brow
(Proposed)
Honley
Robin Hood Tun.

Sough Summit
Entwistle
Ramsbottom
Smithy Bridge
Rochdale E. Junc.
Milnrow
Marsden

Nuttall Tun.
Brooksbottom Tun.
Summerseat
Bromley
Cross
Rochdale
Castleton
E. CE Sidings
S. Castleton Juncs.
New Hey
Standedge Tun. (3m 64 yd)
(Summit)

GREATER
MANCHESTER
Hall i'
Th' Wood
Bury
Bolton
Street
Castleton CE Depot
Shaw
ER
LM
(DIGGLE)

Lostock Junction
(Proposed)
Bolton
BQ
Bury
Heywood
Standard Wagon
Works and
Standard
Railfreight
W.
Derker
Greenfield
Lostock Junc.
Metal Box Co.
Westhoughton
Parcels
Moses
Gate
Radcliffe
Whitefield
Mills
Hill
Mossley
Scout Tun.

C

Daisy Hill
Atherton
Walkden
Moston

Hag
Fold
Patricroft
Victoria
Stalybridge
DERBYSHIRE

MANCHESTER
Piccadilly
Guide Bridge

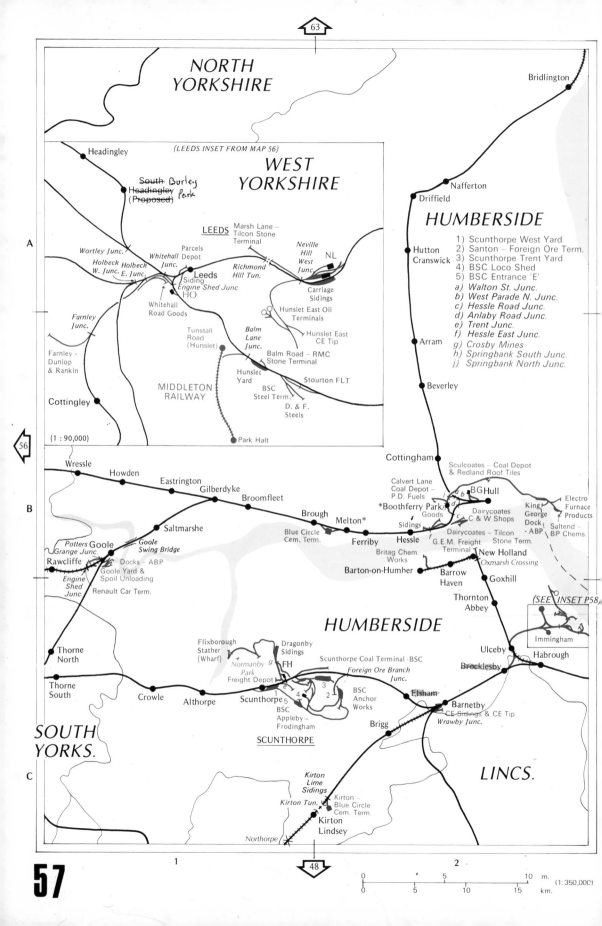

NORTH
YORKSHIRE

Bridlington

Headingley

(LEEDS INSET FROM MAP 56)

WEST
YORKSHIRE

South Burley
Headingley
(Proposed) Park

Nafferton

Driffield

HUMBERSIDE

1) Scunthorpe West Yard
2) Santon – Foreign Ore Term.
3) Scunthorpe Trent Yard
4) BSC Loco Shed
5) BSC Entrance 'E'
a) Walton St. Junc.
b) West Parade N. Junc.
c) Hessle Road Junc.
d) Anlaby Road Junc.
e) Trent Junc.
f) Hessle East Junc.
g) Crosby Mines
h) Springbank South Junc.
j) Springbank North Junc.

LEEDS

Marsh Lane –
Tilcon Stone
Terminal

Neville
Hill
West
Junc.

NL

A

Hutton
Cranswick

Wortley Junc.
Parcels
Depot
*Whitehall
Junc.*
*Holbeck
W. Junc.*
*Holbeck
E. Junc.*
Leeds
Siding
Engine Shed Junc.
HO

*Richmond
Hill Tun.*

Carriage
Sidings

Arram

Whitehall
Road Goods

Hunslet East Oil
Terminals

Beverley

*Farnley
Junc.*

Tunstall
Road
(Hunslet)

*Balm
Lane
Junc.*

Hunslet East
CE Tip

Farnley –
Dunlop
& Rankin

Balm Road – RMC
Stone Terminal

Cottingley

MIDDLETON
RAILWAY

Hunslet
Yard

Stourton FLT

Cottingham

BSC
Steel Term.

D. & F.
Steels

Sculcoates – Coal Depot
& Redland Roof Tiles

(1 : 90,000)

Park Halt

Wressle

Calvert Lane
Coal Depot –
P.D. Fuels

Howden

Eastrington

Gilberdyke

Broomfleet

BG Hull

B

Brough

Melton*

Boothferry Park

Saltmarshe

Blue Circle
Cem. Term.

Goods

King
George
Dock – ABP

Electro
Furnace
Products

Saltend –
BP Chems.

*Potters
Grange Junc.*
Goole

Goole
Swing Bridge

Ferriby

Hessle

Dairycoates
C & W Shops

Dairycoates – Tilcon
Stone Term.

Sidings

Rawcliffe

Docks – ABP

Britag Chem.
Works

G.E.M. Freight
Terminal

New Holland

*Engine
Shed
Junc.*

Goole Yard &
Spoil Unloading

Renault Car Term.

Barton-on-Humber

Barrow
Haven

Oxmarsh Crossing

Goxhill

HUMBERSIDE

Thornton
Abbey

Thorne
North

(SEE INSET P58)

Immingham

Flixborough
Stather
(Wharf)

Dragonby
Sidings

*Normanby
Park*
g
FH
Freight Depot

Scunthorpe Coal Terminal – BSC

*Foreign Ore Branch
Junc.*

Ulceby

Habrough

Thorne
South

Crowle

Althorpe

3

BSC
Anchor
Works

Brocklesby

Elsham

Barnetby

Scunthorpe
1
5
e
4
2

Barnetby
CE Sidings & CE Tip
Wrawby Junc.

SOUTH
YORKS.

BSC
Appleby –
Frodingham

Brigg

SCUNTHORPE

LINCS.

C

Kirton
Lime
Sidings

Kirton Tun.

Kirton –
Blue Circle
Cem. Term.

Northorpe

Kirton
Lindsey

57

2

0   5   10   m.
(1:350,000)
0   5   10   15   km.

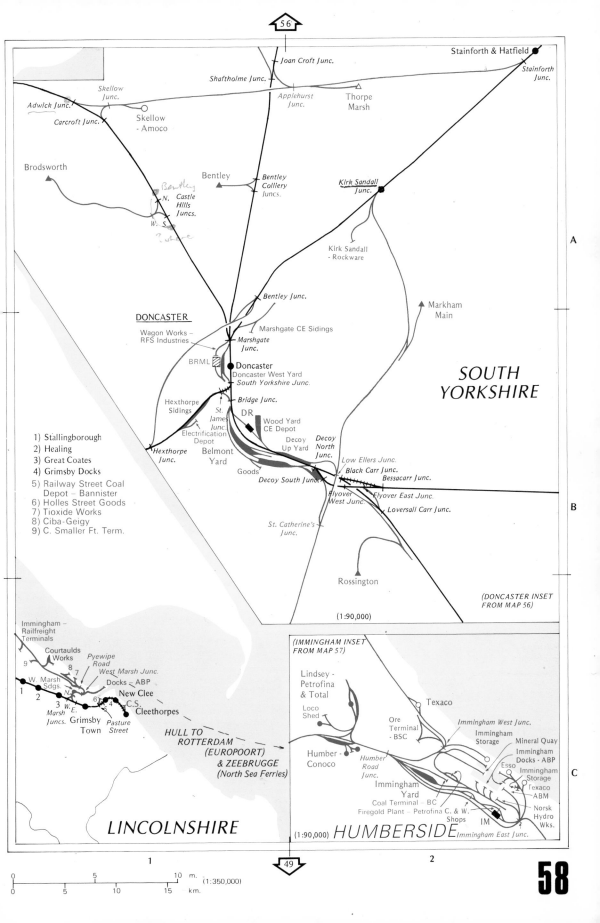

Stainforth & Hatfield
Stainforth Junc.
Joan Croft Junc.
Shaftholme Junc.
Applehurst Junc.
Thorpe Marsh
Skellow Junc.
Adwick Junc.
Skellow - Amoco
Carcroft Junc.
Kirk Sandall Junc.
Brodsworth
Bentley
Bentley Colliery Juncs.
N. Castle Hills Juncs.
W. S.
Kirk Sandall - Rockware

A

Bentley Junc.

Markham Main

DONCASTER
Marshgate CE Sidings
Wagon Works – RFS Industries
Marshgate Junc.
BRML
Doncaster
Doncaster West Yard
South Yorkshire Junc.

SOUTH YORKSHIRE

Hexthorpe Sidings
Bridge Junc.
St. James Junc.
Electrification Depot
Hexthorpe Junc.
Belmont Yard
DR
Wood Yard CE Depot
Decoy Up Yard
Decoy North Junc.
Low Ellers Junc.
Black Carr Junc.
Bessacarr Junc.
Goods
Decoy South Junc.
Flyover West Junc.
Flyover East Junc.
Loversall Carr Junc.

B

St. Catherine's Junc.

1) Stallingborough
2) Healing
3) Great Coates
4) Grimsby Docks
5) Railway Street Coal Depot – Bannister
6) Holles Street Goods
7) Tioxide Works
8) Ciba-Geigy
9) C. Smaller Ft. Term.

Rossington

(DONCASTER INSET FROM MAP 56)

(1:90,000)

Immingham – Railfreight Terminals
Courtaulds Works
Pyewipe Road
West Marsh Junc.
Docks – ABP
New Clee
W. Marsh Sdgs.
N. C.S.
Cleethorpes
W. Marsh Juncs.
W. E.
Grimsby Town
Pasture Street

(IMMINGHAM INSET FROM MAP 57)

Lindsey - Petrofina & Total
Texaco
Loco Shed
Ore Terminal - BSC
Immingham West Junc.
Immingham Storage
Mineral Quay
Humber - Conoco
Humber Road Junc.
Immingham Docks - ABP
Esso
Immingham Yard
Immingham Storage
Coal Terminal – BC
Texaco ABM
Firegold Plant – Petrofina C. & W.
Norsk Hydro Wks.
Shops
IM

C

HULL TO ROTTERDAM (EUROPOORT) & ZEEBRUGGE (North Sea Ferries)

LINCOLNSHIRE

(1:90,000) **HUMBERSIDE** Immingham East Junc.

1

2

0   5   10 m.   (1:350,000)
0   5   10   15 km.

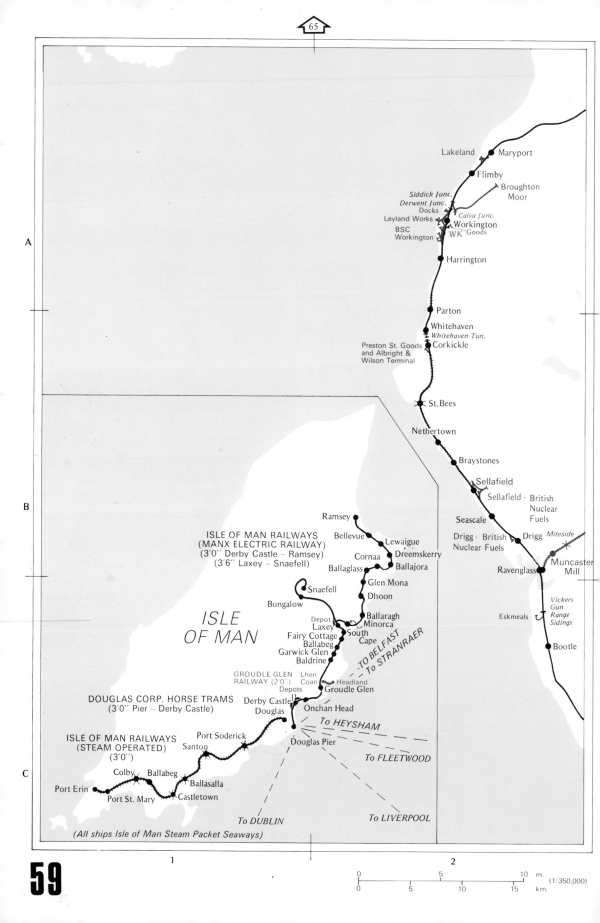

Lakeland ● Maryport
● Flimby
● Broughton
Moor

Siddick Junc.
Derwent Junc.
Docks *Calva Junc.*
Leyland Works
BSC ● Workington
Workington WK Goods

A

● Harrington

● Parton
Whitehaven
Whitehaven Tun.
Preston St. Goods ● Corkickle
and Albright &
Wilson Terminal

● St. Bees

Nethertown

Braystones

Sellafield
Sellafield · British
Nuclear Fuels

Seascale

Drigg · British Drigg *Miteside*
Nuclear Fuels

Ramsey ●
Bellevue Lewaigue
Cornaa Dreemskerry
Ballaglass Ballajora

ISLE OF MAN RAILWAYS
(MANX ELECTRIC RAILWAY)
(3'0" Derby Castle – Ramsey)
(3'6" Laxey – Snaefell)

Glen Mona Ravenglass Muncaster
Dhoon Mill

Snaefell
Bungalow Ballaragh *Vickers*
Depot Minorca Eskmeals *Gun*
Laxey South *Range*
Fairy Cottage Cape *Sidings*
ISLE Ballabeg
OF MAN Garwick Glen
Baldrine

B

● Bootle

TO BELFAST
To STRANRAER

GROUDLE GLEN Lhen
RAILWAY (2'0") Coan Headland
Depots Groudle Glen

DOUGLAS CORP. HORSE TRAMS
(3'0" Pier – Derby Castle)
Derby Castle
Douglas Onchan Head

To HEYSHAM

ISLE OF MAN RAILWAYS Port Soderick
(STEAM OPERATED) Santon Douglas Pier
(3'0")
Colby Ballabeg *To FLEETWOOD*
Port Erin Ballasalla
Port St. Mary Castletown

C

To DUBLIN *To LIVERPOOL*

(All ships Isle of Man Steam Packet Seaways)

59

1   2

0   5   10 m.
0   5   10   15 km.
(1:350,000)

Aspatria

Baron Wood No. 2 Tun.
Baron Wood No. 1 Tun.

Lazonby &
Kirkoswald

Lazonby Tun.

Langwathby

*Culgaith
Tunnel*

Penrith

*Waste Bank
Tun.*

Newbiggin British
Gypsum Wks.

A

Pooley Bridge

KESWICK
Landing
Stage

DERWENT
WATER

*(Ullswater
Navigation &
Transit Co.)*

ULLSWATER

Hawse End

Low Brandelhow   Ashness Gate

High Brandelhow   Lodore

Howtown

Harrison's
Sidings–ARC

*(Keswick
Launch)*

Glenridding

BSC Hardendale
Quarry

CUMBRIA

Shap–
Ribblesdale
Cement

Shap Summit (916ft)

Shap Granite
– T.W. Ward
(Disused)

61

Ambleside

B

Beckfoot   Eskdale
(Dalegarth)

Irton
Road   *Fisherground*

Black   The Green
Bridge

Windermere

Staveley

RAVENGLASS & ESKDALE
RAILWAY (1´3´´)

Coniston

Far
Sawrey   Bowness
Bowness

Burneside

*(National
Trust)*   CONISTON

Kendal

WINDERMERE

Park-a-Moor

Oxenholme
Lake District

*(Windermere Iron
Steamboat Company)*

CE
Sidings   CE
Shed   *Carnforth
East
Junc.*

LAKESIDE & HAVERTHWAITE
RAILWAY

Lakeside

*Carnforth
F. & M.
Junc.*   R. O. Hodgson

Newby Bridge   *Carnforth Stn. Junc.*

Foxfield

Haverthwaite   Steamtown   Carnforth

Green Road

(1:90,000)

Silecroft

Kirkby-in
Furness

*Kent
Viaduct*

Plumpton Junc.   *Leven
Viaduct*   Grange-over-
Sands

Millom

Askam   Teeside Farmers
Oils Ltd.   Ulverston   Cark &
Cartmel   Arnside

Glaxochem
Works

LANCS.

C

Park South Junc.   Kents
Bank   Silverdale

Lindal Tun.   Dalton   *Melling
Tun.*

Dalton Tun.
Dalton Junc.   Carnforth   *(SEE INSET ABOVE)*

1   **54**   2

0   5   10   m.   *(1:350,000)*
0   5   10   15   km.   **60**

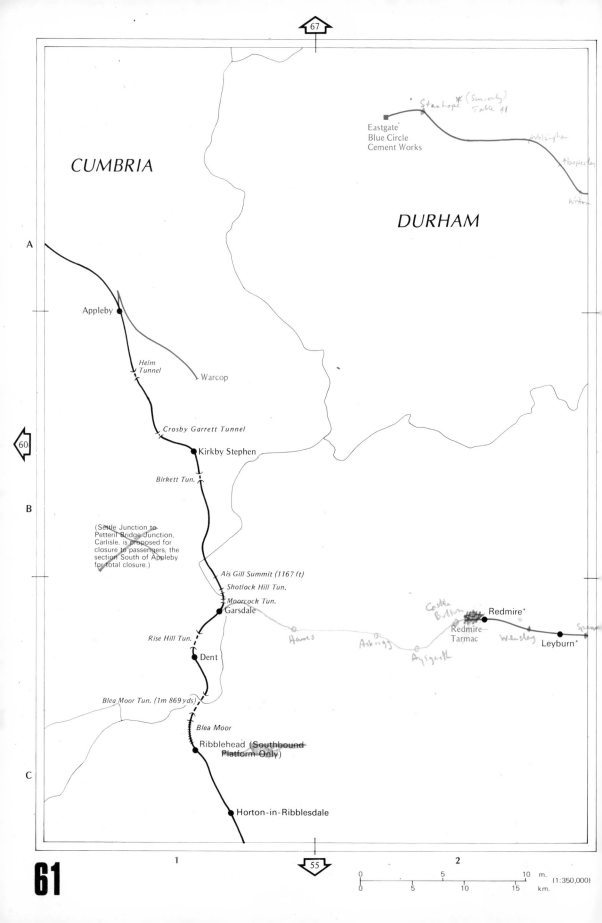

CUMBRIA

DURHAM

Eastgate
Blue Circle
Cement Works

Stanhope (Sun. only)
Table 41

Wolsingham

Harperley

Witton

A

Appleby

Warcop

Helm
Tunnel

Crosby Garrett Tunnel

Kirkby Stephen

Birkett Tun.

B

(Settle Junction to
Petteril Bridge Junction,
Carlisle, is proposed for
closure to passengers, the
section South of Appleby
for total closure.)

Ais Gill Summit (1167 ft)

Shotlock Hill Tun.

Moorcock Tun.
Garsdale

Rise Hill Tun.

Dent

Blea Moor Tun. (1m 869 yds)

Blea Moor

Ribblehead (Southbound
Platform Only)

Castle
Bolton

Redmire

Redmire—
Tarmac

Wensley

Leyburn

Spenn

Hawes

Askrigg

Aysgarth

C

Horton-in-Ribblesdale

1

60

55

2

0   5   10   m.
0   5   10   15   km.

(1:350,000)

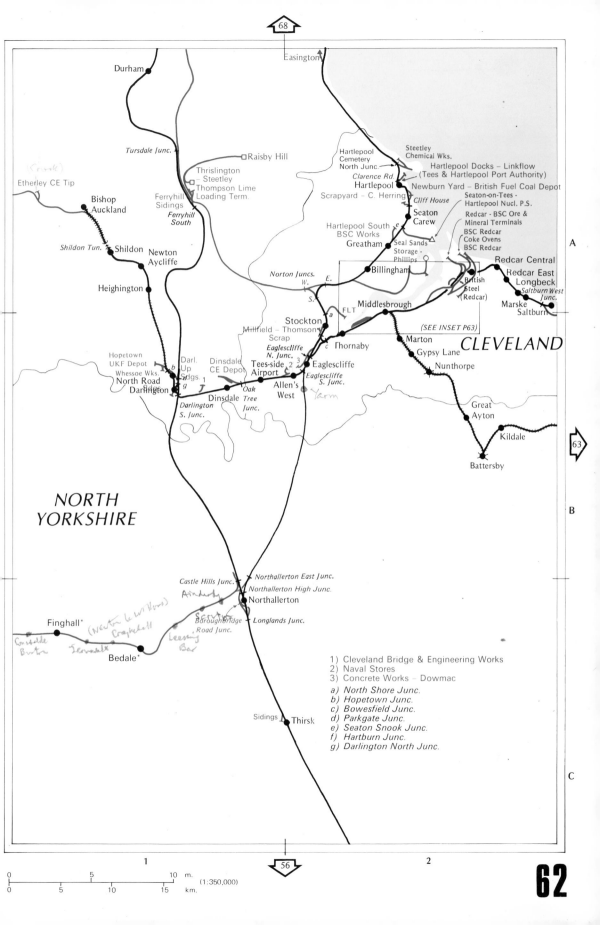

Easington

Durham

Tursdale Junc.

Raisby Hill

(Crooke)

Etherley CE Tip

Thrislington – Steetley
Thompson Lime
Loading Term.

Bishop
Auckland

Ferryhill
Sidings

Ferryhill
South

Shildon Tun.   Shildon

Newton
Aycliffe

Heighington

Hartlepool
Cemetery
North Junc.

Steetley
Chemical Wks.

Hartlepool Docks – Linkflow
(Tees & Hartlepool Port Authority)

Clarence Rd.

Hartlepool

Newburn Yard – British Fuel Coal Depot

Scrapyard – C. Herring

Cliff House

Seaton-on-Tees –
Hartlepool Nucl. P.S.

Seaton
Carew

Redcar – BSC Ore &
Mineral Terminals
BSC Redcar
Coke Ovens
BSC Redcar

Hartlepool South
BSC Works

Greatham

Seal Sands
Storage –
Phillips

e

Redcar Central

Redcar East

Longbeck

British
Steel
(Redcar)

Billingham

Norton Juncs.

W.

E.

S.

Saltburn West
Junc.

Marske

Saltburn

A

Middlesbrough

FLT

a

(SEE INSET P63)

CLEVELAND

Stockton

Millfield – Thomson
Scrap

Eaglescliffe
N. Junc.

c

Thornaby

Marton

Gypsy Lane

Nunthorpe

Hopetown
UKF Depot
Whessoe Wks.
North Road
Darlington

Darl.
Up
Sidgs.

b

g

Dinsdale
CE Depot

Tees-side
Airport

2 3

Eaglescliffe

Eaglescliffe
S. Junc.

1

Oak
Tree
Junc.

Allen's
West

Yarm

Darlington
S. Junc.

Dinsdale

Great
Ayton

Kildale

63

Battersby

**NORTH
YORKSHIRE**

B

Finghall*

(Newton le Willows)
Crakehall

Constable
Burton   Leonards

Ainderby

Scruton

Leeming
Bar

Castle Hills Junc.

Bedale*

Boroughbridge
Road Junc.

Northallerton East Junc.

Northallerton High Junc.

Northallerton

Longlands Junc.

1) Cleveland Bridge & Engineering Works
2) Naval Stores
3) Concrete Works – Dowmac

a) North Shore Junc.
b) Hopetown Junc.
c) Bowesfield Junc.
d) Parkgate Junc.
e) Seaton Snook Junc.
f) Hartburn Junc.
g) Darlington North Junc.

Sidings   Thirsk

C

1   56   2

0   5   10 m.
0   5   10   15 km.
(1:350,000)

62

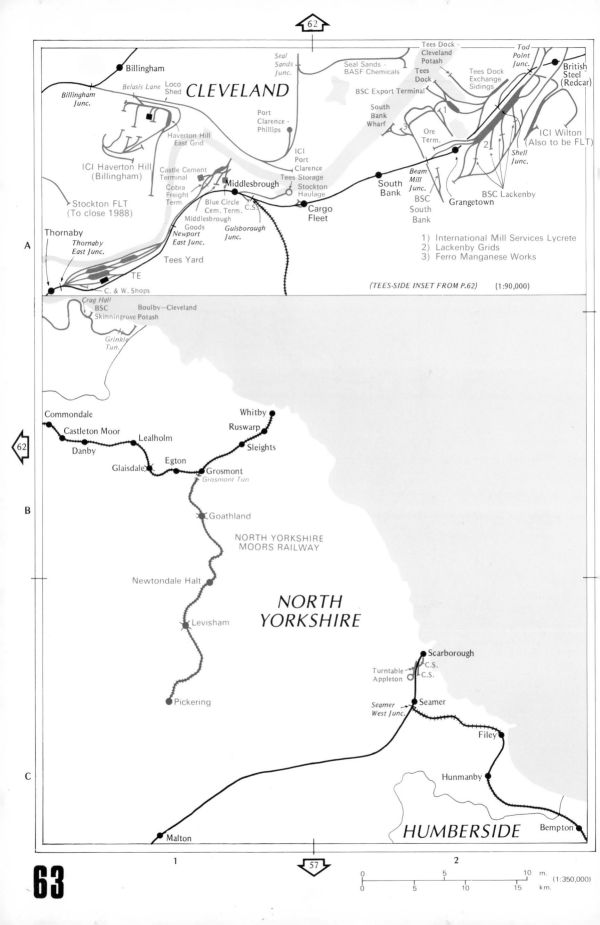

Billingham

Belasis Lane   Loco
Shed

Billingham Junc.

CLEVELAND

Seal Sands Junc.

Seal Sands -
BASF Chemicals

Tees Dock -
Cleveland
Potash

Tees
Dock

*Tod
Point
Junc.*

British
Steel
(Redcar)

BSC Export Terminal

Tees Dock Exchange
Sidings

Haverton Hill
East Grid

Port
Clarence -
Phillips

South
Bank Wharf

ICI
Port
Clarence

Ore
Term.

1

ICI Wilton
(Also to be FLT)

ICI Haverton Hill
(Billingham)

Castle Cement
Terminal

Cobra
Freight
Term.

Blue Circle
Cem. Term.

Middlesbrough

Tees Storage
Stockton Haulage

2

*Shell
Junc.*

*Beam
Mill
Junc.*

Stockton FLT
(To close 1988)

Middlesbrough
Goods

*Newport
East Junc.*

C.S.

*Guisborough
Junc.*

Cargo
Fleet

South
Bank

BSC
South
Bank

BSC Lackenby

Grangetown

Thornaby

*Thornaby
East Junc.*

Tees Yard

TE

1) International Mill Services Lycrete
2) Lackenby Grids
3) Ferro Manganese Works

3

C. & W. Shops

A

Crag Hall
BSC
Skinningrove Potash

Boulby—Cleveland

(TEES-SIDE INSET FROM P.62)   (1:90,000)

*Grinkle
Tun.*

Commondale

Castleton Moor

Danby

Lealholm

Glaisdale

Egton

Whitby

Ruswarp

Sleights

Grosmont

62

Grosmont Tun.

B

Goathland

**NORTH YORKSHIRE
MOORS RAILWAY**

Newtondale Halt

*NORTH
YORKSHIRE*

Levisham

Scarborough

C.S.
C.S.

Turntable
Appleton

Pickering

*Seamer
West Junc.*

Seamer

Filey

C

Hunmanby

Bempton

Malton

HUMBERSIDE

0   5   10 m.
(1:350,000)
0   5   10   15 km.

Dalrymple Junc.

SC (WATERSIDE)
BC
Chalmerston
(Proposed)

Maybole

Kilkerran

STRATHCLYDE

A

Girvan

Pinmore Tun.
& Summit

Pinwherry

Barrhill

65

Chirmorie
Summit

B

Glenwhilly

To LARNE (P. & O.)

Cairnryan

To LARNE (Sealink) & To
DOUGLAS (I. of M. S.P.
Seaways)

**DUMFRIES &
GALLOWAY**

Stranraer
Harbour

Stranraer
Town

Stockton
Haulage

Dunragit

C

1

2

0   5   10 m.
          (1:350,000)
0   5   10   15 km.

64

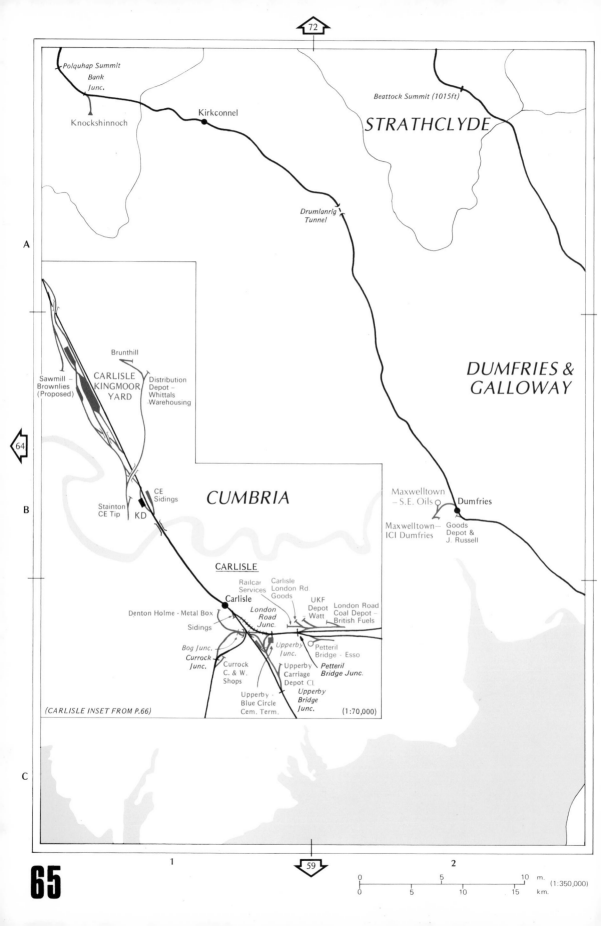

Polquhap Summit
Bank
Junc.

Knockshinnoch

Kirkconnel

Beattock Summit (1015ft)

STRATHCLYDE

Drumlanrig
Tunnel

A

**DUMFRIES &
GALLOWAY**

Brunthill

Sawmill –
Brownlies
(Proposed)

**CARLISLE
KINGMOOR
YARD**

Distribution
Depot –
Whittals
Warehousing

64

CE
Sidings

CUMBRIA

Stainton
CE Tip

KD

B

Maxwelltown
– S.E. Oils

Dumfries

Maxwelltown –
ICI Dumfries

Goods
Depot &
J. Russell

CARLISLE

Railcar
Services

Carlisle
London Rd.
Goods

UKF
Depot
Watt

London Road
Coal Depot –
British Fuels

Carlisle

*London
Road
Junc.*

Denton Holme - Metal Box

Sidings

Bog Junc.

*Currock
Junc.*

Currock
C. & W.
Shops

Upperby
Carriage
Depot Cl

*Upperby
Junc.*

Petteril
Bridge - Esso

*Petteril
Bridge Junc.*

Upperby -
Blue Circle
Cem. Term.

*Upperby
Bridge
Junc.*

(CARLISLE INSET FROM P.66)

(1:70,000)

C

1

59

2

0   5   10   m.
                              (1:350,000)
0   5   10   15   km.

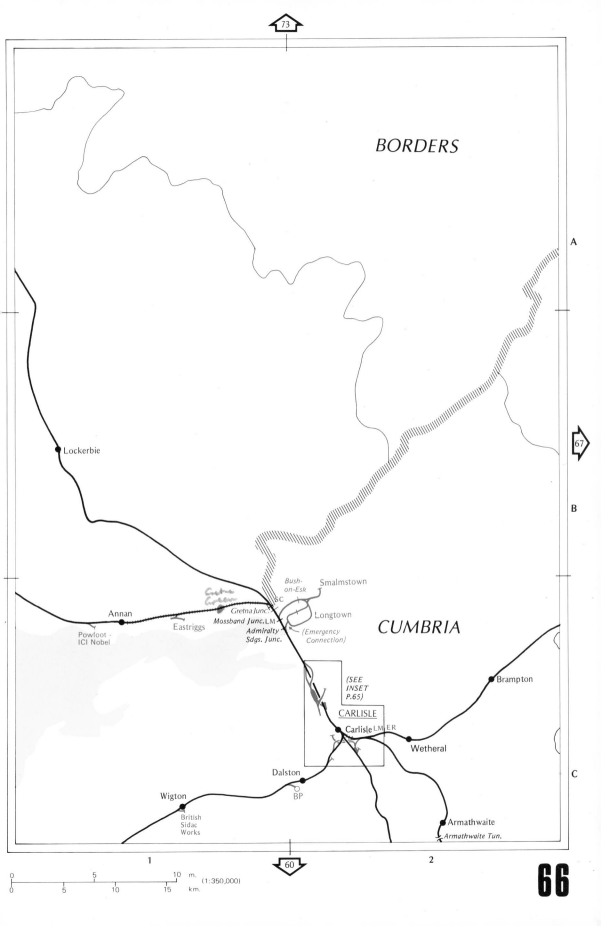

BORDERS

Lockerbie

67

Annan
Powfoot -
ICI Nobel
Eastriggs

Gretna Green
SC
Gretna Junc.
Bush-on-Esk Smalmstown
Mossband Junc. LM
Longtown
Admiralty Sdgs. Junc.
(Emergency Connection)

CUMBRIA

(SEE INSET P.65)

CARLISLE

Carlisle LM ER
Wetheral

Brampton

C

Dalston
BP

Wigton
British
Sidac
Works

Armathwaite
Armathwaite Tun.

A

B

1

2

0   5   10 m.
0   5   10   15 km.
(1:350,000)

66

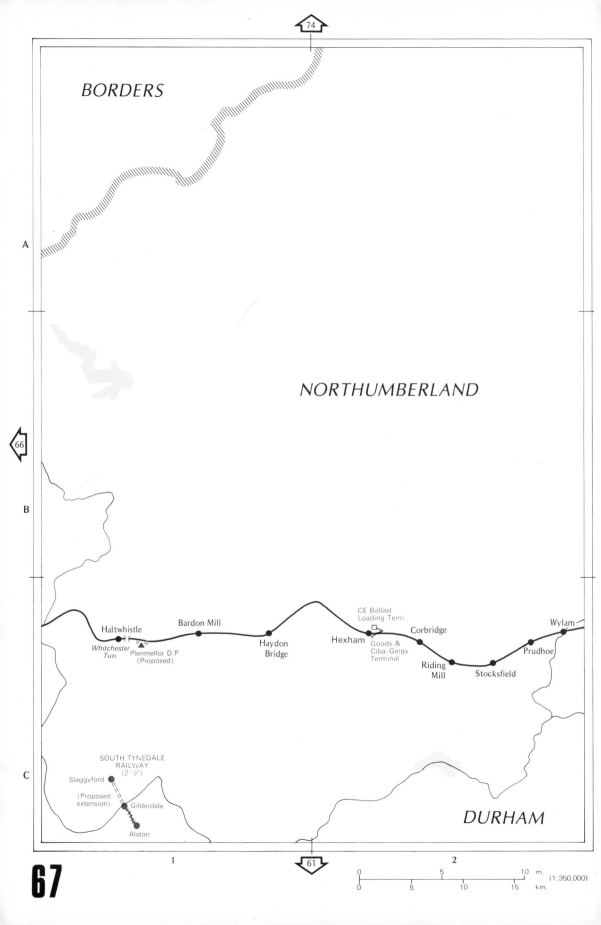

BORDERS

NORTHUMBERLAND

66

A

B

Haltwhistle

Bardon Mill

Whitchester Tun. Plenmellor D.P. (Proposed)

Haydon Bridge

CE Ballast Loading Term.

Hexham Goods & Ciba-Geigy Terminal

Corbridge

Wylam

Prudhoe

Riding Mill

Stocksfield

C

SOUTH TYNEDALE RAILWAY (2' 0")

Slaggyford

(Proposed extension)

Gilderdale

Alston

DURHAM

1   2

0   5   10 m.
                              (1:350,000)
0   5   10   15 km.

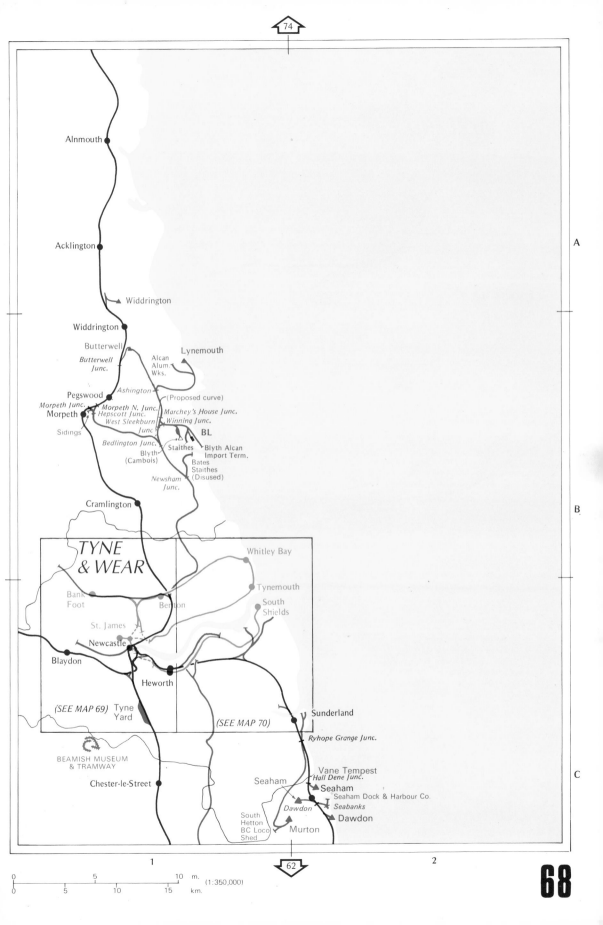

Alnmouth

Acklington

A

Widdrington

Widdrington

Butterwell

Butterwell
Junc.

Lynemouth

Alcan
Alum.
Wks.

Pegswood

Ashington

(Proposed curve)

Morpeth Junc.
Morpeth

Morpeth N. Junc.

Hepscott Junc.

Marchey's House Junc.

West Sleekburn
Junc.

Winning Junc.

Sidings

BL

Bedlington Junc.

Blyth
(Cambois)

Staithes

Blyth Alcan
Import Term.

Bates
Staithes
(Disused)

Newsham
Junc.

Cramlington

B

TYNE
& WEAR

Whitley Bay

Bank
Foot

Tynemouth

Benton

South
Shields

St. James

Newcastle

Blaydon

Heworth

(SEE MAP 69) Tyne
Yard

(SEE MAP 70)

Sunderland

Ryhope Grange Junc.

BEAMISH MUSEUM
& TRAMWAY

Vane Tempest

Hall Dene Junc.

C

Chester-le-Street

Seaham

Seaham

Seaham Dock & Harbour Co.

Dawdon

Seabanks

South
Hetton
BC Loco
Shed

Dawdon

Murton

1

2

0   5   10 m.   (1:350,000)

0   5   10   15 km.

68

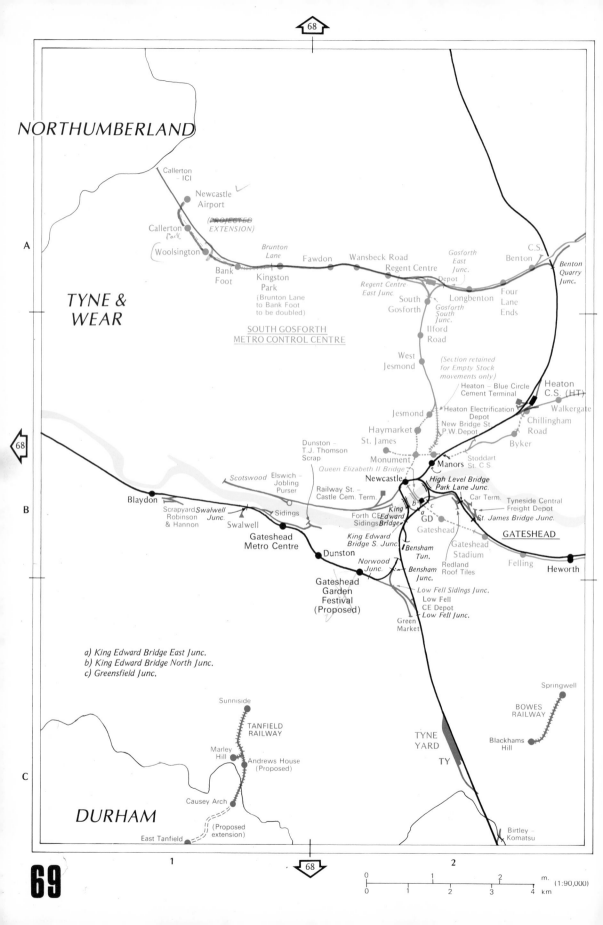

NORTHUMBERLAND

A

TYNE &
WEAR

68

B

a) King Edward Bridge East Junc.
b) King Edward Bridge North Junc.
c) Greensfield Junc.

DURHAM

C

Callerton – ICI

Newcastle
Airport

Callerton
(PROJECTED
EXTENSION)

Woolsington

Bank
Foot

Kingston
Park
(Brunton Lane
to Bank Foot
to be doubled)

Brunton
Lane

Fawdon

Wansbeck Road

Regent Centre

Regent Centre
East Junc.

South
Gosforth

Gosforth
East
Junc.

Depot

Gosforth
South
Junc.

Ilford
Road

C.S.

Benton

Benton
Quarry
Junc.

Longbenton

Four
Lane
Ends

SOUTH GOSFORTH
METRO CONTROL CENTRE

West
Jesmond

(Section retained
for Empty Stock
movements only)

Heaton – Blue Circle
Cement Terminal

Heaton
C.S. (HT)

Walkergate

Jesmond

Heaton Electrification
Depot
New Bridge St.
P.W.Depot

Chillingham
Road

Byker

Haymarket
St. James

Dunston –
T.J. Thomson
Scrap

Queen Elizabeth II Bridge

Monument

Manors

Stoddart
St. C.S.

Newcastle

High Level Bridge
Park Lane Junc.

Scotswood

Elswich –
Jobling
Purser

Railway St. –
Castle Cem. Term.

b

Car Term.

Tyneside Central
Freight Depot

St. James Bridge Junc.

GATESHEAD

Blaydon

Scrapyard
Robinson
& Hannon

Swalwell
Junc.

Sidings

Swalwell

King
Edward
Bridge

Forth CE
Sidings

a

GD

Gateshead

Gateshead
Stadium

Redland
Roof Tiles

Felling

Heworth

Gateshead
Metro Centre

Dunston

King Edward
Bridge S. Junc.

Norwood
Junc.

Bensham
Tun.

Bensham
Junc.

Gateshead
Garden
Festival
(Proposed)

Green
Market

Low Fell Sidings Junc.

Low Fell
CE Depot
Low Fell Junc.

Sunniside

TANFIELD
RAILWAY

Marley
Hill

Andrews House
(Proposed)

Causey Arch

(Proposed
extension)

East Tanfield

TYNE
YARD

TY

Springwell

BOWES
RAILWAY

Blackhams
Hill

Birtley –
Komatsu

1

68

2

0   1   2   m. (1:90,000)
0   1   2   3   4   km

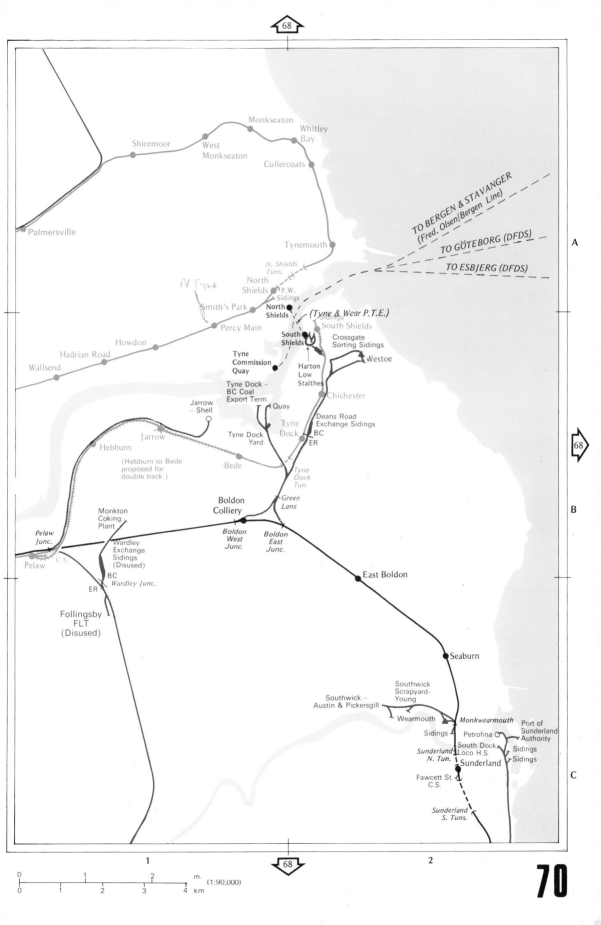

Monkseaton
Whitley Bay
Shiremoor
West Monkseaton
Cullercoats
Palmersville
Tynemouth

TO BERGEN & STAVANGER
(Fred. Olsen/Bergen Line)
TO GÖTEBORG (DFDS)
TO ESBJERG (DFDS)

A

N. Shields Tuns.
N Tyne
North Shields
P.W. Sidings
Smith's Park
North Shields
Percy Main
(Tyne & Wear P.T.E.)
Sidings
South Shields
Crossgate Sorting Sidings
South Shields
Howdon
Hadrian Road
Wallsend
Tyne Commission Quay
Harton Low Staithes
Westoe
Chichester
Tyne Dock – BC Coal Export Term.
Quay
Jarrow – Shell
Deans Road Exchange Sidings
Jarrow
Tyne Dock
BC
Hebburn
Tyne Dock Yard
ER
Bede
(Hebburn to Bede proposed for double track.)
Tyne Dock Tun.

B

Pelaw Junc.
Monkton Coking Plant
Boldon Colliery
Green Lane
Wardley Exchange Sidings (Disused)
Boldon West Junc.
Boldon East Junc.
Pelaw
C.S.
BC
ER
Wardley Junc.
Follingsby FLT (Disused)
East Boldon

Seaburn

Southwick Scrapyard- Young
Southwick – Austin & Pickersgill
Wearmouth
Monkwearmouth
Port of Sunderland Authority
Sidings
Petrofina
Sidings
South Dock
Sidings
Sunderland N. Tun.
Loco H.S.
Sunderland
Fawcett St. C.S.

C

Sunderland S. Tuns.

1
2

0   1   2   m.   (1:90,000)
0   1   2   3   4   km

70

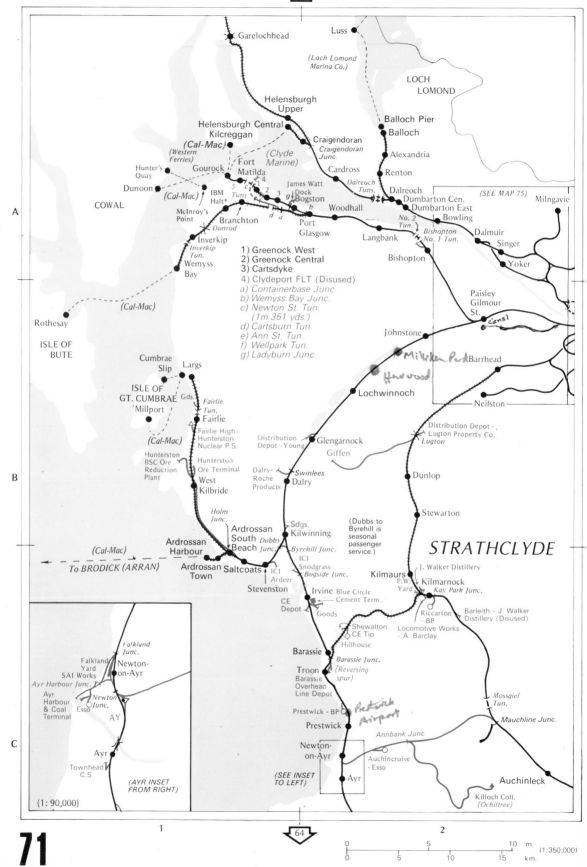

Garelochhead

Luss

(Loch Lomond Marina Co.)

LOCH LOMOND

Helensburgh Upper

Balloch Pier
Balloch

Helensburgh Central
Kilcreggan

Craigendoran
Craigendoran Junc.

Alexandria

(Western Ferries)

(Clyde Marine)

Cardross

Renton

Hunter's Quay

Gourock

Fort Matilda
4

Dunoon

(Cal-Mac)

James Watt Dock
Bogston

IBM Halt*

5 Tuns
c
2
3
g
b

Dalreoch Tuns.

Dalreoch

(SEE MAP 75)

Milngavie

COWAL

McInroy's Point

Branchton
Dunrod

d a

Woodhall

Dumbarton Cen.
Dumbarton East
Bowling

Dalmuir
Singer

Port Glasgow

No. 2 Tun.

Yoker

Langbank

Bishopton No. 1 Tun.

Inverkip

Inverkip Tun.

Bishopton

Paisley Gilmour St.

Wemyss Bay

Rothesay

(Cal-Mac)

1) Greenock West
2) Greenock Central
3) Cartsdyke
4) Clydeport FLT (Disused)
a) *Containerbase Junc.*
b) *Wemyss Bay Junc.*
c) *Newton St. Tun.*
   (1m.351 yds.)
d) *Cartsburn Tun.*
e) *Ann St. Tun.*
f) *Wellpark Tun.*
g) *Ladyburn Junc.*

Johnstone

Canal

Barrhead

ISLE OF BUTE

Milliken Park
Harwood

Lochwinnoch

Neilston

Cumbrae Slip

Largs

ISLE OF GT. CUMBRAE
'Millport'

Gds.

Fairlie Tun.

Fairlie

Fairlie High-
Hunterston Nuclear P.S.

Distribution Depot - Young

Glengarnock
Giffen

Distribution Depot -
Lugton Property Co.
Lugton

(Cal-Mac)

Hunterston BSC Ore Reduction Plant

Hunterston Ore Terminal

West Kilbride

Dalry-Roche Products

Swinlees
Dalry

Dunlop

Stewarton

Holm Junc.

Ardrossan South Beach

Dubbs Junc.

Sdgs.
Kilwinning

Byrehill Junc.

(Dubbs to Byrehill is seasonal passenger service.)

STRATHCLYDE

(Cal-Mac)

Ardrossan Harbour

To BRODICK (ARRAN)

Ardrossan Town

Saltcoats

ICI Ardeer

ICI Snodgrass
Bogside Junc.

Kilmaurs

J. Walker Distillery

P.W. Yard

Kilmarnock
Kay Park Junc.

Stevenston

Irvine

Blue Circle Cement Term.

CE Depot
Goods

Riccarton - BP

Locomotive Works - A. Barclay

Barleith - J. Walker Distillery (Disused)

Shewalton CE Tip
Hillhouse

Barassie

Barassie Junc.
(Reversing spur)

Troon

Barassie Overhead Line Depot

Mossgiel Tun.

Prestwick - BP

Prestwick Airport

Mauchline Junc.

Prestwick

Annbank Junc.

Newton-on-Ayr

Auchincruive - Esso

Ayr

Auchinleck

Killoch Coll. *(Ochiltree)*

(SEE INSET TO LEFT)

Falkland Junc.

Falkland Yard
SAI Works

Newton-on-Ayr

Ayr Harbour Junc.

Ayr Harbour & Coal Terminal

Esso

Newton Junc.

AY

Ayr

Townhead C.S.

(AYR INSET FROM RIGHT)

(1: 90,000)

1

2

0   5   10 m.
|————|————|————|————|
0   5   10   15 km.

(1:350,000)

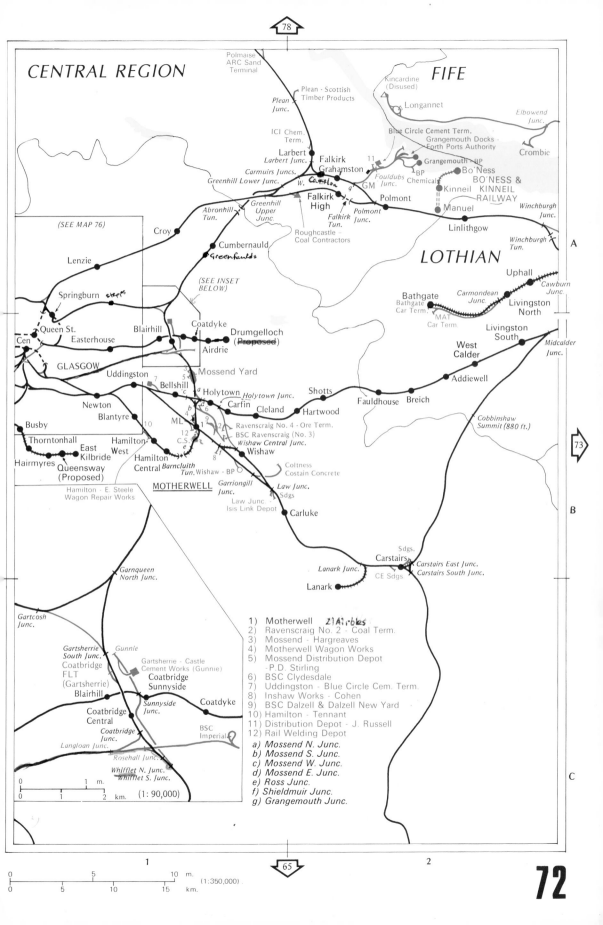

CENTRAL REGION

FIFE

Polmaise
ARC Sand
Terminal

Plean - Scottish
Timber Products

Kincardine
(Disused)

Longannet

Elbowend
Junc.

Plean
Junc.

ICI Chem.
Term.

Blue Circle Cement Term.

Grangemouth Docks -
Forth Ports Authority

Crombie

Larbert

Larbert Junc.

Falkirk
Grahamston

Grangemouth - BP

11

BO'NESS &
KINNEIL
RAILWAY

Carmuirs Juncs.

BP
Chemicals

Bo'Ness

Greenhill Lower Junc.

W. Castlon

GM

Kinneil

Abronhill
Tun.

Greenhill
Upper Junc.

Falkirk
High

Polmont

Manuel

Winchburgh
Junc.

Croy

Greenhill Lower Junc.

Falkirk
Tun.

Polmont
Junc.

Linlithgow

Winchburgh
Tun.

A

(SEE MAP 76)

Cumbernauld

Greenfaulds

Roughcastle -
Coal Contractors

LOTHIAN

Lenzie

(SEE INSET
BELOW)

Uphall

Cawburn
Junc.

Springburn

steps

Bathgate

Carmondean
Junc.

Livingston
North

Queen St.

Coatdyke

Drumgelloch
(Proposed)

Bathgate
Car Term.

MAT
Car Term.

Cen

Blairhill

Livingston
South

Easterhouse

Airdrie

West
Calder

Midcalder
Junc.

GLASGOW

Mossend Yard

Uddingston

7

Bellshill

Holytown

a

Holytown Junc.

Shotts

Addiewell

Newton

c

Carfin

Cleland

Hartwood

Fauldhouse

Breich

Cobbinshaw
Summit (880 ft.)

Blantyre

b
d

Busby

10

e

ML

Thorntonhall

Hamilton
West

12

C.S.

1

2

Ravenscraig No. 4 - Ore Term.
BSC Ravenscraig (No. 3)

73

East
Kilbride

Hamilton
Central

Barncluith
Tun.

Wishaw Central Junc.

Hairmyres

Wishaw - BP

Wishaw

Coltness
Costain Concrete

Queensway
(Proposed)

MOTHERWELL

Garriongill
Junc.

Law Junc.
Sdgs

Hamilton - E. Steele
Wagon Repair Works

Law Junc. -
Isis Link Depot

Carluke

B

Garnqueen
North Junc.

Lanark Junc.

Carstairs

Sdgs.

Carstairs East Junc.
Carstairs South Junc.

Gartcosh
Junc.

CE Sdgs.

Lanark

Gartsherrie
South Junc.

Gunnie

Coatbridge
FLT
(Gartsherrie)

Gartsherrie - Castle
Cement Works (Gunnie)

Coatbridge
Sunnyside

Blairhill

Coatbridge
Central

Sunnyside
Junc.

Coatdyke

Coatbridge
Junc.

BSC
Imperial

Langloan Junc.

Rosehall Junc.

Whifflet N. Junc.
Whifflet S. Junc.

0   1   m.
0   1   2   km.   (1: 90,000)

1) Motherwell 2)Airbles
2) Ravenscraig No. 2 - Coal Term.
3) Mossend - Hargreaves
4) Motherwell Wagon Works
5) Mossend Distribution Depot
   - P.D. Stirling
6) BSC Clydesdale
7) Uddingston - Blue Circle Cem. Term.
8) Inshaw Works - Cohen
9) BSC Dalzell & Dalzell New Yard
10) Hamilton - Tennant
11) Distribution Depot - J. Russell
12) Rail Welding Depot

a) Mossend N. Junc.
b) Mossend S. Junc.
c) Mossend W. Junc.
d) Mossend E. Junc.
e) Ross Junc.
f) Shieldmuir Junc.
g) Grangemouth Junc.

0   5   10   m.
0   5   10   15   km.   (1:350,000)

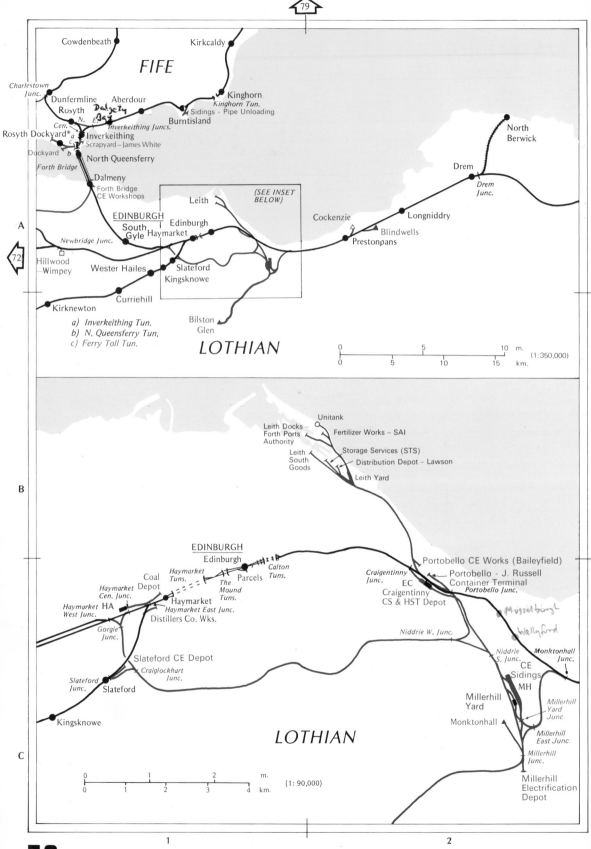

Cowdenbeath
Kirkcaldy

FIFE

Charlestown
Junc.
Dunfermline   Aberdour   Kinghorn
Rosyth   Dalgety   Kinghorn Tun.
Cen.   N.   East   Sidings - Pipe Unloading
Rosyth Dockyard* a   Inverkeithing Juncs.   Burntisland
Inverkeithing
Scrapyard – James White
Dockyard b
North Queensferry
Forth Bridge
Dalmeny
Forth Bridge
CE Workshops   Leith   (SEE INSET
BELOW)   Cockenzie   Longniddry

North
Berwick

Drem

Drem
Junc.

EDINBURGH
South   Edinburgh
Gyle   Haymarket

A

Newbridge Junc.   Prestonpans   Blindwells

72

Hillwood
Wimpey   Wester Hailes   Slateford
Kingsknowe

Curriehill

Kirknewton

a) Inverkeithing Tun.
b) N. Queensferry Tun.
c) Ferry Toll Tun.

Bilston
Glen

LOTHIAN

0   5   10 m.
0   5   10   15 km.
(1:350,000)

B

Leith Docks –
Forth Ports
Authority

Unitank
Fertilizer Works – SAI
Storage Services (STS)
Distribution Depot – Lawson

Leith
South
Goods

Leith Yard

EDINBURGH
Edinburgh   Calton
Haymarket   Parcels   Tuns.
Tuns.   The
Mound
Coal   Tuns.
Depot
Haymarket
Cen. Junc.   Haymarket
Haymarket HA   Haymarket East Junc.
West Junc.   Distillers Co. Wks.
Gorgie
Junc.

Portobello CE Works (Baileyfield)
Craigentinny   Portobello - J. Russell
Junc.   Container Terminal
EC   Portobello Junc.
Craigentinny
CS & HST Depot

Niddrie W. Junc.

Mussel burgh
Wallyford

Slateford CE Depot
Craiglockhart
Junc.   Niddrie
S. Junc.   Monktonhall
Junc.
Slateford
Junc.   Slateford   CE
Sidings
MH
Kingsknowe   Millerhill
Yard   Millerhill
Yard
Junc.
Monktonhall

Millerhill
East Junc.

Millerhill
Junc.

LOTHIAN

0   1   2   m.
0   1   2   3   4 km.
(1: 90,000)

C

Millerhill
Electrification
Depot

1   2

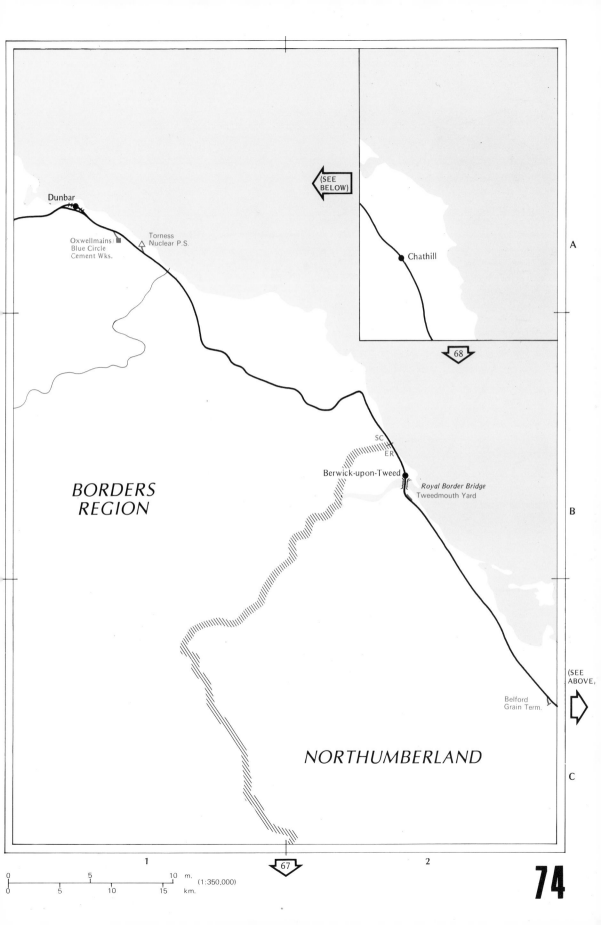

Dunbar

Oxwellmains
Blue Circle
Cement Wks.

Torness
Nuclear P.S.

(SEE
BELOW)

Chathill

A

68

SC
ER

Berwick-upon-Tweed

Royal Border Bridge
Tweedmouth Yard

BORDERS
REGION

B

(SEE
ABOVE,

Belford
Grain Term.

NORTHUMBERLAND

C

1

0   5   10 m.
0   5   10   15 km.   (1:350,000)

67

2

74

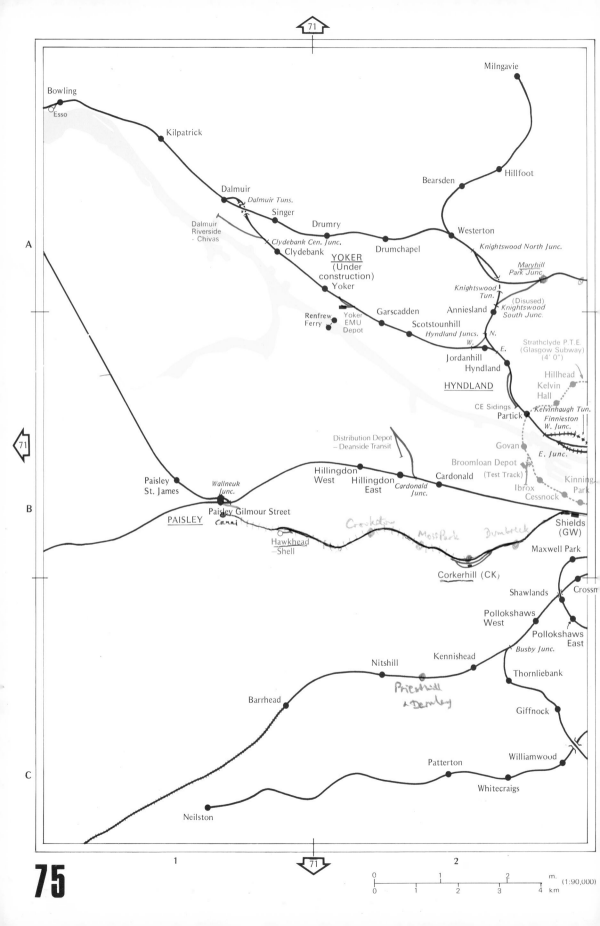

Milngavie

Bowling
Esso

Kilpatrick

Bearsden

Hillfoot

Dalmuir
Dalmuir Tuns.
Singer
Drumry
Westerton
Knightswood North Junc.

Dalmuir
Riverside
- Chivas
Clydebank Cen. Junc.
Clydebank
Drumchapel
*Maryhill
Park Junc.*

YOKER
(Under
construction)
Yoker
Garscadden
Scotstounhill
Anniesland
*Knightswood
Tun.*
(Disused)
Knightswood
South Junc.

A

Renfrew
Ferry
Yoker
EMU
Depot
Hydland Juncs. N.
W.
Jordanhill
Hyndland
E.
Strathclyde P.T.E.
(Glasgow Subway)
(4' 0")

HYNDLAND
Hillhead
Kelvin
Hall

CE Sidings
Kelvinhaugh Tun.
Partick
*Finnieston
W. Junc.*

Distribution Depot
– Deanside Transit
Govan
E. Junc.
Broomloan Depot
(Test Track)

Paisley
St. James
*Wallneuk
Junc.*
Hillingdon
West
Hillingdon
East
Cardonald
*Cardonald
Junc.*
Ibrox
Cessnock
Kinning
Park

B

PAISLEY
Canal
Paisley Gilmour Street
Shields
(GW)

Hawkhead
–Shell
Crookston
MossPark
Dumbreck
Maxwell Park

Corkerhill (CK)
Shawlands
Crossm

Pollokshaws
West
Pollokshaws
East

Nitshill
Kennishead
Busby Junc.
Thornliebank

Pricehill
↳Darnley

Barrhead
Giffnock

Williamwood

C

Patterton
Whitecraigs

Neilston

0   1   2   m. (1:90,000)
0   1   2   3   4 km

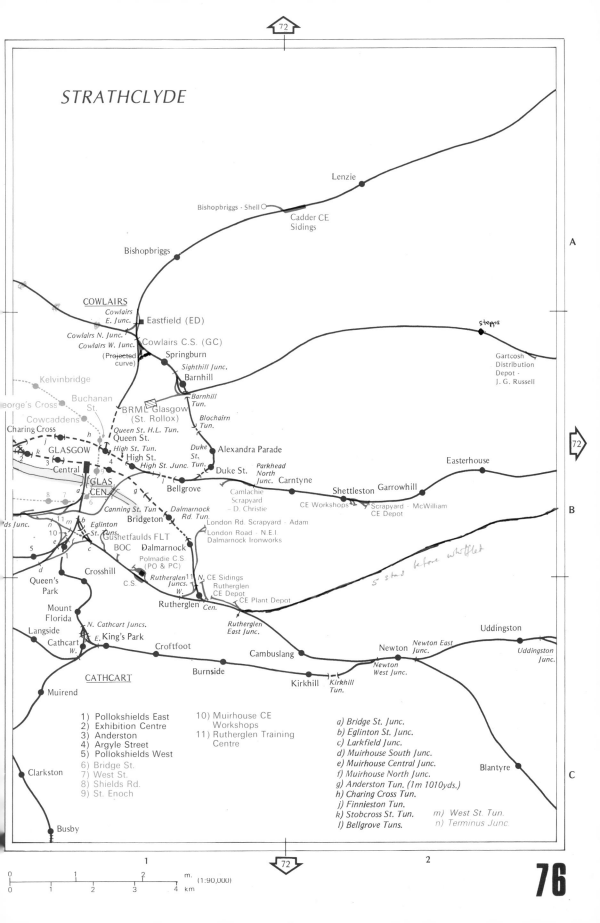

STRATHCLYDE

Lenzie

Bishopbriggs - Shell

Cadder CE
Sidings

Bishopbriggs

A

COWLAIRS
Cowlairs
E. Junc.   Eastfield (ED)
Cowlairs N. Junc.
Cowlairs W. Junc. Cowlairs C.S. (GC)
(Projected   Springburn
curve)
Sighthill Junc.
Barnhill

Stepps

Gartcosh
Distribution
Depot -
J. G. Russell

Kelvinbridge

Buchanan
St.
Barnhill
eorge's Cross   BRML Glasgow   *Tun.*
Cowcaddens   (St. Rollox)
Charing Cross   *Queen St. H.L. Tun.*   *Blochairn*
Queen St.   *Tun.*
h   *High St. Tun.*   *Duke*
GLASGOW   *j*   *St.*   Alexandra Parade
k   High St.   *Tun.*
2 Central   *High St. Junc.*   Duke St.   *Parkhead*
North
GLAS   Bellgrove   *Junc.* Carntyne   Shettleston   Garrowhill
CEN.   *g*   Camlachie
Scrapyard   CE Workshops
Canning St. Tun   – D. Christie   Scrapyard - McWilliam
Bridgeton   *Dalmarnock*   CE Depot
ds Junc.   *n* *m b* Eglinton   *Rd. Tun.*   London Rd. Scrapyard - Adam
10   *St. Tuns.*   London Road - N.E.I
e *f* Gushetfaulds FLT   Dalmarnock Ironworks
5   *c*   BOC   Dalmarnock
1   Polmadie C.S.
d   Crosshill   (PO & PC)
Queen's   *C.S.* *Rutherglen* 11   N. CE Sidings
Park   *Juncs.*   Rutherglen
Mount   *W.*   CE Depot
Florida   Rutherglen *Cen.*   CE Plant Depot
Langside   *N. Cathcart Juncs.*   *Rutherglen*
Cathcart   *E.* King's Park   *East Junc.*
W.   Croftfoot   Cambuslang
CATHCART

Easterhouse

B

5 stnd before whtflet

Uddingston

Newton *Newton East*
Junc.   *Uddingston*
Junc.
Newton
West Junc.
Burnside   Kirkhill *Kirkhill*
Tun.

Muirend

Blantyre

C

Clarkston

Busby

1) Pollokshields East
2) Exhibition Centre
3) Anderston
4) Argyle Street
5) Pollokshields West
6) Bridge St.
7) West St.
8) Shields Rd.
9) St. Enoch

10) Muirhouse CE
Workshops
11) Rutherglen Training
Centre

a) Bridge St. Junc.
b) Eglinton St. Junc.
c) Larkfield Junc.
d) Muirhouse South Junc.
e) Muirhouse Central Junc.
f) Muirhouse North Junc.
g) Anderston Tun. (1m 1010yds.)
h) Charing Cross Tun.
j) Finnieston Tun.
k) Stobcross St. Tun.   m) West St. Tun.
l) Bellgrove Tuns.   n) Terminus Junc.

1   2

0   1   2   m. (1:90,000)
0 1 2 3 4 km

76

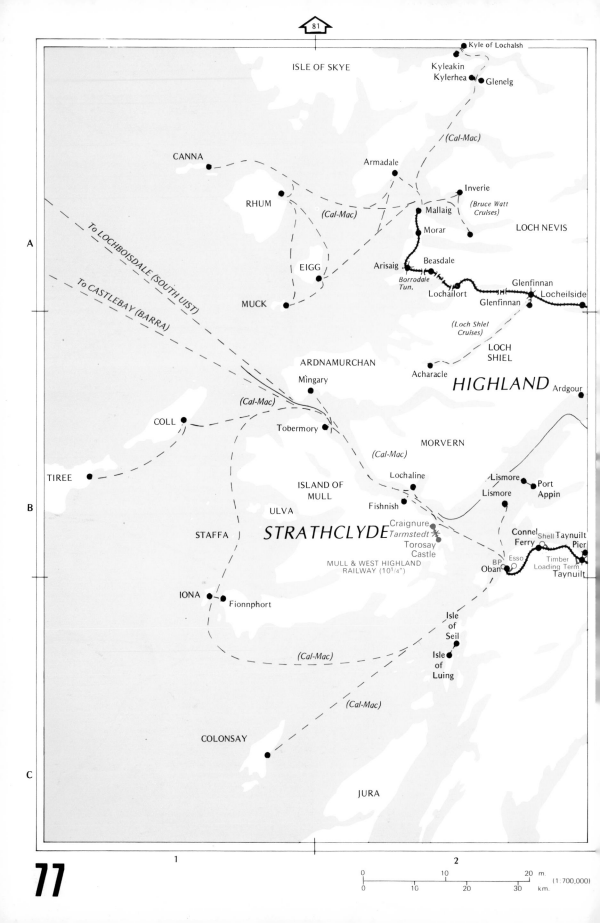

ISLE OF SKYE

Kyle of Lochalsh

Kyleakin
Kylerhea • Glenelg

(Cal-Mac)

CANNA

(Cal-Mac)

RHUM

Armadale

Inverie

Mallaig

(Bruce Watt Cruises)

LOCH NEVIS

Morar

A

EIGG

Arisaig
Beasdale

Borrodale Tun.

Lochailort

Glenfinnan • Locheilside

Glenfinnan

MUCK

(Loch Shiel Cruises)

LOCH SHIEL

ARDNAMURCHAN

Acharacle

HIGHLAND Ardgour

To LOCHBOISDALE (SOUTH UIST)

Mingary

(Cal-Mac)

To CASTLEBAY (BARRA)

COLL

Tobermory

MORVERN

(Cal-Mac)

Lismore • Port Appin

Lismore

TIREE

ISLAND OF MULL

Lochaline

B

ULVA

Fishnish

STAFFA

STRATHCLYDE

Craignure
Tarmstedt
Torosay
Castle

Connel Ferry

Shell Taynuilt
Pier

MULL & WEST HIGHLAND
RAILWAY (10¼″)

BP
Esso

Timber
Loading Term.

IONA

Fionnphort

Oban

Taynuilt

Isle
of
Seil

Isle
of
Luing

(Cal-Mac)

(Cal-Mac)

COLONSAY

C

JURA

1

2

0   10   20 m.

0   10   20   30 km.

(1:700,000)

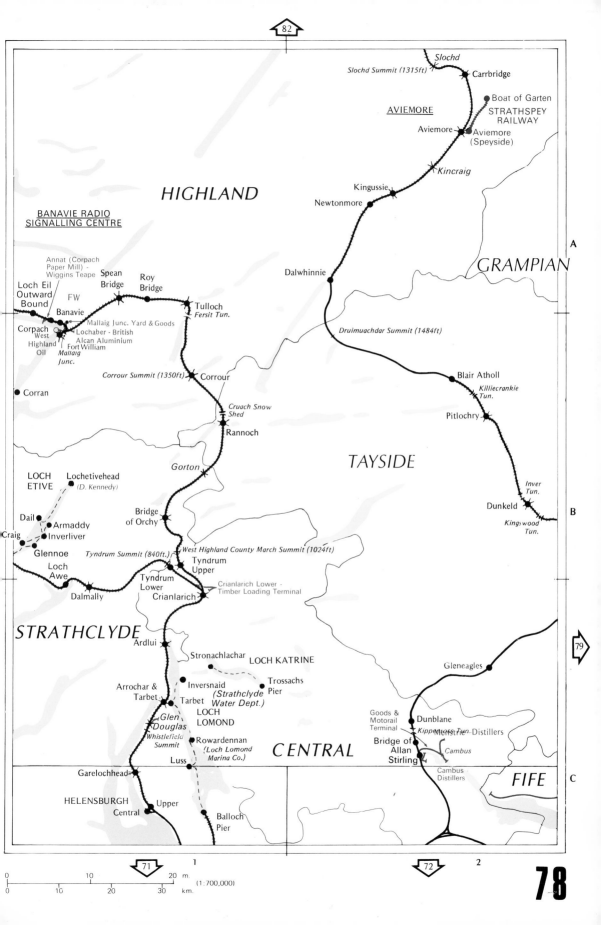

Slochd
Slochd Summit (1315ft) — Carrbridge
● Boat of Garten
STRATHSPEY
RAILWAY
AVIEMORE
Aviemore
● Aviemore (Speyside)
Kincraig
Kingussie
Newtonmore

HIGHLAND

GRAMPIAN

A

Dalwhinnie

BANAVIE RADIO
SIGNALLING CENTRE

Annat (Corpach Paper Mill) - Wiggins Teape
Spean Bridge
Roy Bridge
Loch Eil Outward Bound
FW
Banavie
Tulloch
Fersit Tun.
Corpach
West Highland Oil
Mallaig Junc. Yard & Goods
Lochaber - British Alcan Aluminium
Fort William
Mallaig Junc.

Druimuachdar Summit (1484ft)

Blair Atholl
Killiecrankie Tun.

Pitlochry

● Corran

Corrour Summit (1350ft) — Corrour

Cruach Snow Shed
● Rannoch

TAYSIDE

Gorton

Inver Tun.
Dunkeld
B

LOCH ETIVE
Lochetivehead *(D. Kennedy)*
● Dail
● Armaddy
● Inverliver
Craig ●
● Glennoe
Bridge of Orchy
Kingswood Tun.

Loch Awe
Tyndrum Summit (840ft.)
West Highland County March Summit (1024ft)
Tyndrum Upper
Dalmally
Tyndrum Lower
Crianlarich
Crianlarich Lower - Timber Loading Terminal

STRATHCLYDE

Ardlui

Stronachlachar
LOCH KATRINE
Gleneagles
79

Arrochar & Tarbet
Inversnaid
Trossachs Pier
(Strathclyde Water Dept.)
Tarbet
LOCH LOMOND
Goods & Motorail Terminal
Dunblane
Kippenross Tun. Distillers
Glen Douglas
Whistlefield Summit
Rowardennan
(Loch Lomond Marina Co.)
Bridge of Allan
Stirling
Cambus

CENTRAL

Garelochhead
Luss
Cambus Distillers

FIFE
C

HELENSBURGH
Central Upper
Balloch Pier

1
2

0 10 20 m.
0 10 20 30 km.
(1:700,000)

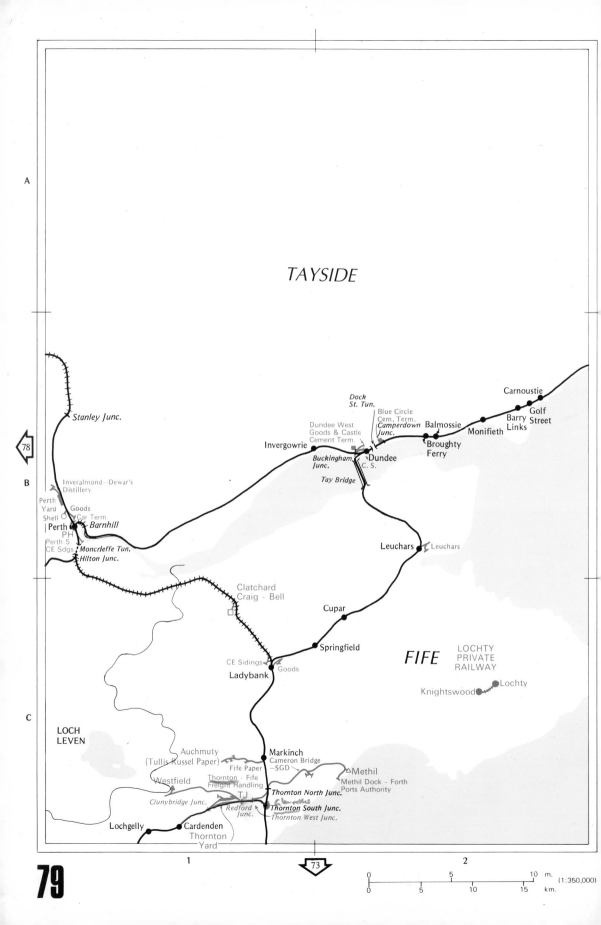

TAYSIDE

Stanley Junc.

78

Inveralmond – Dewar's
Distillery

Perth
Yard
Shell
Goods
Car Term
Perth
PH
Perth S
CE Sdgs
Barnhill
Moncrieffe Tun.
Hilton Junc.

*Dock
St. Tun.*
Blue Circle
Cem. Term.
*Camperdown
Junc.*
Dundee West
Goods & Castle
Cement Term.
Invergowrie
*Buckingham
Junc.*
Dundee
C. S.
Tay Bridge

Carnoustie
Golf
Street
Barry
Links
Monifieth
Balmossie
Broughty
Ferry

Leuchars — Leuchars

Clatchard
Craig - Bell

Cupar

Springfield

FIFE   LOCHTY
PRIVATE
RAILWAY

CE Sidings
Goods
Ladybank

Knightswood — Lochty

C

LOCH
LEVEN

Auchmuty
(Tullis Russel Paper)
Markinch
Cameron Bridge
–SGD
Fife Paper
Methil
Methil Dock - Forth
Ports Authority
Westfield
Thornton - Fife
Freight Handling
Clunybridge Junc.
TJ
Thornton North Junc.
Redford
Junc.
Thornton South Junc.
Thornton West Junc.
Lochgelly
Cardenden
Thornton
Yard

79

1

73

2

0   5   10 m.
0   5   10   15   km.
(1:350,000)

A

B

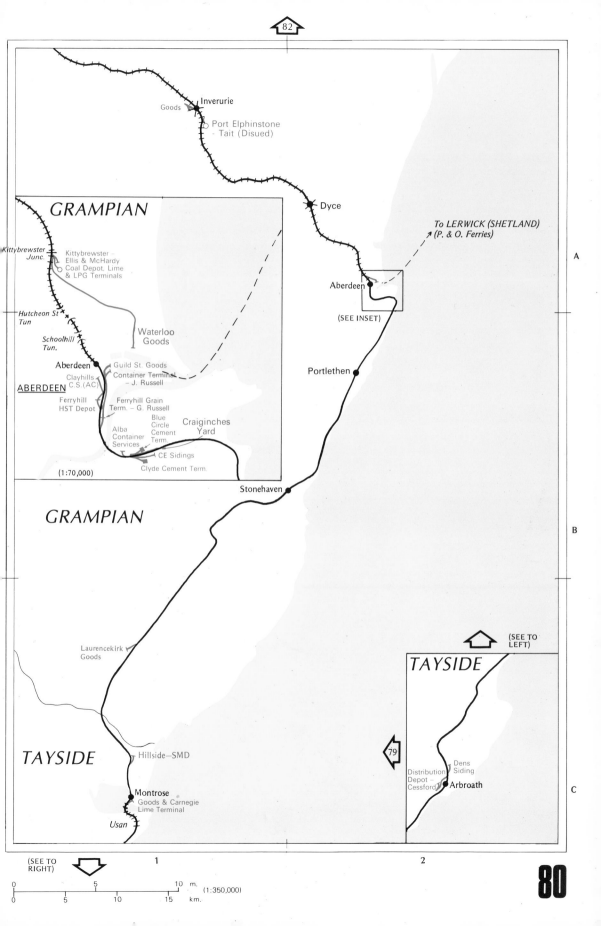

Goods
Inverurie
Port Elphinstone
- Tait (Disued)

Dyce

To LERWICK (SHETLAND)
(P. & O. Ferries)

A

Aberdeen

(SEE INSET)

GRAMPIAN

Kittybrewster
Junc.
Kittybrewster –
Ellis & McHardy
Coal Depot, Lime
& LPG Terminals

Hutcheon St
Tun.

Schoolhill
Tun.

Waterloo
Goods

Aberdeen
Guild St. Goods
Container Terminal
– J. Russell
Clayhills
C.S.(AC)

ABERDEEN

Ferryhill
HST Depot
Ferryhill Grain
Term. – G. Russell
Blue
Circle
Cement
Term.
*Craiginches
Yard*
Alba
Container
Services
CE Sidings
Clyde Cement Term.

(1:70,000)

Portlethen

Stonehaven

GRAMPIAN

B

Laurencekirk
Goods

(SEE TO
LEFT)

TAYSIDE

79

TAYSIDE

Hillside–SMD

Dens
Siding
Distribution
Depot –
Cessford
Arbroath

C

Montrose
Goods & Carnegie
Lime Terminal

Usan

(SEE TO
RIGHT)

1

2

0   5   10 m.
                           (1:350,000)
0   5   10   15   km.

80

ISLE OF LEWIS

A

Kylestrome

Kylesku

To STORNOWAY (Cal-Mac)

B

Ullapool

HIGHLAND

ISLE OF SKYE

Ravens Rock
Summit (458 ft)

Lochluichart

Achanalt

Garve

Corriemoillie
Summit (429 ft)

Achnasheen

Dingwall

C

Luib Summit (646 ft)

Muir of Ord
Grain Term

ISLE OF RAASAY

Achnashellach

Strathcarron

Attadale

Beauly

Sconser

Plockton

Stromeferry

Duirinish

Duncraig

Kyle of Lochalsh

1

2

77

0   10   20   m.

0   10   20   30   km.

(1 : 700,000)

81

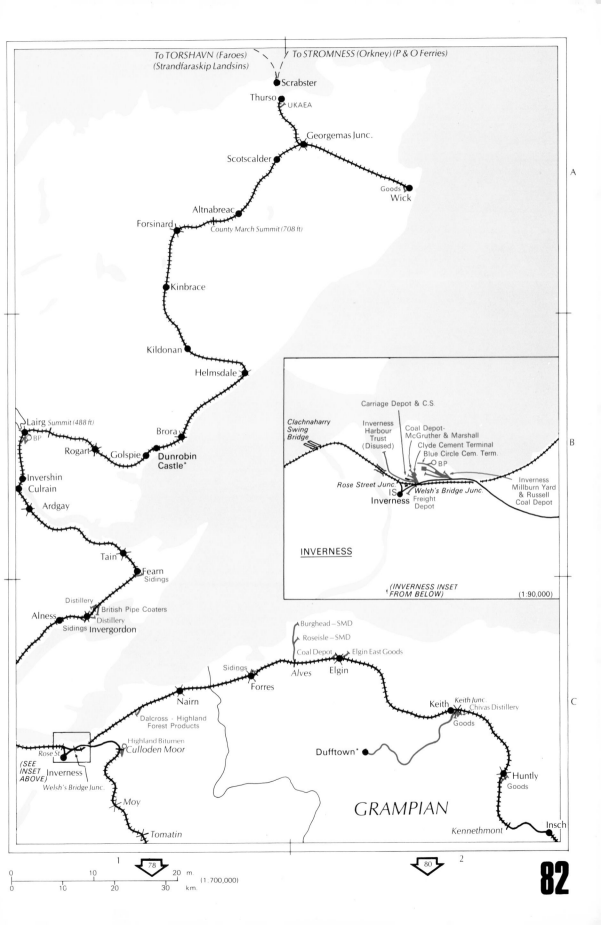

To TORSHAVN (Faroes)
(Strandfaraskip Landsins)

To STROMNESS (Orkney) (P & O Ferries)

Scrabster
Thurso
UKAEA
Georgemas Junc.
Scotscalder
Goods
Wick
Altnabreac
Forsinard
County March Summit (708 ft)
Kinbrace
Kildonan
Helmsdale

Lairg *Summit (488 ft)*
BP
Rogart
Golspie
Brora
Dunrobin Castle*
Invershin
Culrain
Ardgay
Tain
Fearn
Sidings
Distillery
British Pipe Coaters
Distillery
Alness
Sidings Invergordon

Clachnaharry
Swing
Bridge

Carriage Depot & C.S.
Inverness
Harbour
Trust
(Disused)
Coal Depot-
McGruther & Marshall
Clyde Cement Terminal
Blue Circle Cem. Term.
BP
Rose Street Junc.
IS
Inverness
Welsh's Bridge Junc.
Freight
Depot
Inverness
Millburn Yard
& Russell
Coal Depot

INVERNESS

(INVERNESS INSET FROM BELOW)
(1:90,000)

Burghead – SMD
Roseisle – SMD
Coal Depot
Elgin East Goods
Sidings
Forres
Alves
Elgin
Nairn
Keith
Keith Junc.
Chivas Distillery
Goods
Dalcross - Highland
Forest Products
Highland Bitumen
Rose St
Culloden Moor
(SEE
INSET
ABOVE)
Inverness
Dufftown*
Welsh's Bridge Junc.
Moy
Huntly
Goods
GRAMPIAN
Tomatin
Kennethmont
Insch

0   10   20 m.
0   10   20   30   km.
(1.700,000)

1   78   2   80

82

√ = new

ARAN ISLANDS

(C.I.E.)

GALWAY

Kilronan (INISHMORE)

INISHMAAN

INISHEER

Gort*

LOUGH DERG

CLARE

Cloughjordan

Bell Line Cont. Term.

Guinness Term.

Burmah

Limerick

Goods

Limerick Wagon Works

Sdgs

Limerick Check

(LIMERICK INSET FROM RIGHT)

(1:180,000)

A

Ennis

Goods & Container Terminal

Goods

Silvermines Junc.

Nenagh

Silvermines

Birdhill

Kilmastulla Shale Siding

Templemore

Goods

Thurles

Ore Terminals

Castlemungret Cement Works

Limerick

Killonan Junc.

Dromkeen

Sugar Factory – Comhlucht Siuicre Eireann Teo

Foynes

Ballingrane Junc.

(SEE INSET TO LEFT)

Milltown Crossing

LIMERICK

Keane's Points

Limerick Junction

P. W. Sdgs.

Kyle Crossing

Tipperary

Newcastle West

Knocklong*

P.W. Depot

Cahir

(Ballingrane Junc. to Tralee is disused)

Barnargh Tun.

Kilmallock*

Sidings

GREAT SOUTHERN RAILWAY PRESERVATION SOCIETY (PROPOSED)

Rathluirc (Charleville)

Goods

Fenit

Goods

Buttevant

Kilfenora

Tralee

Spa

P.W. Sidings Great Southern Railway Pres. Soc. √

Farranfore

Goods

Goods & Container Terminal

Mallow

Killarney Junc.

KERRY

Rathmore

Banteer

B

Goods

Goods

Millstreet

Goods

Killarney

Cobh Junction

Mogeely*

(SEE INSET BELOW)

Midleton*

Youghal*

CORK

Cork

Carrigaloe

Rushbrooke

Cobh

Cork (Ringaskiddy)

To SWANSEA (Swansea – Cork Ferries)

To ROSCOFF (Brittany Ferries) & LE HAVRE (Irish Cont. Line.)

C

Cork Tun.

C.S. Sdgs.

Cork

Gds.

Cont. Term.

Burmah

Tivoli Container Terminal Cork Harbour Commissioners (Dart Line)

North Esk Container Terminal

Cobh Junction

Little Island

Fota

Guinness Terminal

Marino Point – Nitrigin Eireann Teo

Ammonia

Fertiliser

(1:180,000)

(CORK INSET FROM ABOVE)

Carrigaloe

83

1

2

0   15   30   m.

(1:1,070,000)

0   15   30   45 km.

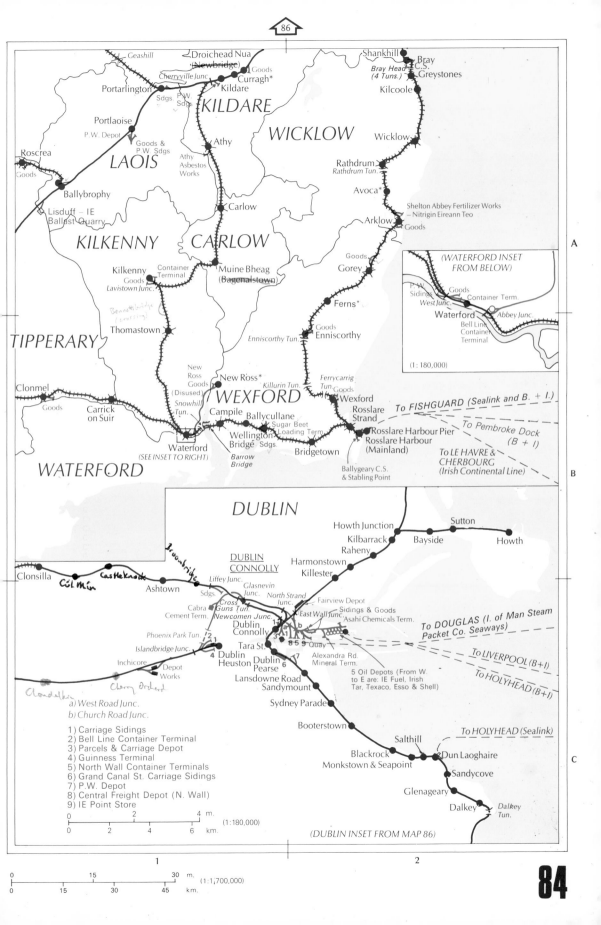

Geashill
Droichead Nua
(Newbridge)
Shankhill
Bray
Goods
C.S.
Curragh*
Bray Head
Greystones
Cherryville Junc.
(4 Tuns.)
Kildare
Kilcoole
Portarlington
Sdgs.
P.W.
Sdgs.
KILDARE
Portlaoise
WICKLOW
Wicklow
P.W. Depot
Athy
Goods &
P.W. Sdgs
Roscrea
LAOIS
Athy
Rathdrum
Goods
Asbestos
Rathdrum Tun.
Works
Ballybrophy
Avoca*
Carlow
Lisduff – IE
Shelton Abbey Fertilizer Works
Ballast Quarry
– Nitrigin Eireann Teo
Arklow
KILKENNY
CARLOW
Goods
Kilkenny
Muine Bheag
Container
(Bagenalstown)
Gorey
Terminal
Goods
Lavistown Junc.

(WATERFORD INSET
FROM BELOW)

A

P.W.
Sidings
Goods
Container Term.
West Junc.
Bennettsbridge
(crossing)
Ferns*
Waterford
Abbey Junc.
Thomastown
Bell Line
Enniscorthy
Goods
Container
Enniscorthy
Terminal
TIPPERARY
Enniscorthy Tun.
(1 : 180,000)

New
Ross
Goods
Ferrycarrig
Clonmel
New Ross*
Tun.
Goods
Killurin Tun.
TO FISHGUARD (Sealink and B. + I.)
(Disused)
WEXFORD
Wexford
Carrick
Snowhill
Campile
Rosslare
To Pembroke Dock
on Suir
Tun.
Ballycullane
Strand
(B + I)
Goods
Sugar Beet
Rosslare Harbour Pier
Wellington
Loading Term.
Rosslare Harbour
To LE HAVRE &
Bridge
Sdgs.
(Mainland)
CHERBOURG
Bridgetown
(Irish Continental Line)
Waterford
Barrow
(SEE INSET TO RIGHT)
Bridge
WATERFORD
Ballygeary C.S.
& Stabling Point

B

DUBLIN

Sutton
Howth Junction
Bayside
Kilbarrack
Howth
Raheny
Clonsilla
Broombridge
Harmonstown
Cúl Mín
Castleknock
Liffey Junc.
Killester
Ashtown
Glasnevin
DUBLIN
Junc.
North Strand
CONNOLLY
Sdgs.
Junc.
Cabra
Cross
Fairview Depot
Cement Term.
Guns Tun.
Sidings & Goods
Newcomen Junc.
Asahi Chemicals Term.
To DOUGLAS (I. of Man
Dublin
Steam Packet Co. Seaways)
Phoenix Park Tun.
Connolly
Islandbridge Junc.
Tara St.
Quay
Inchicore
Dublin
Alexandra Rd.
To LIVERPOOL (B+I)
Heuston
Dublin
Mineral Term.
Depot
Pearse
To HOLYHEAD (B+I)
Works
Lansdowne Road
5 Oil Depots (From W.
Clondalkin
Cherry Orchard
Sandymount
to E are: IE Fuel, Irish
Tar, Texaco, Esso & Shell)
Sydney Parade

a) West Road Junc.
b) Church Road Junc.
Booterstown
To HOLYHEAD (Sealink)
1) Carriage Sidings
Salthill
2) Bell Line Container Terminal
Blackrock
Dun Laoghaire
3) Parcels & Carriage Depot
Monkstown & Seapoint
4) Guinness Terminal
Sandycove
5) North Wall Container Terminals
6) Grand Canal St. Carriage Sidings
Glenageary
7) P.W. Depot
8) Central Freight Depot (N. Wall)
Dalkey
Dalkey
9) IE Point Store
Tun.
0
2
4 m.
(1:180,000)
0
2
4
6 km.
(DUBLIN INSET FROM MAP 86)

C

1
2

0
15
30 m.
(1:1,700,000)
0
15
30
45 km.

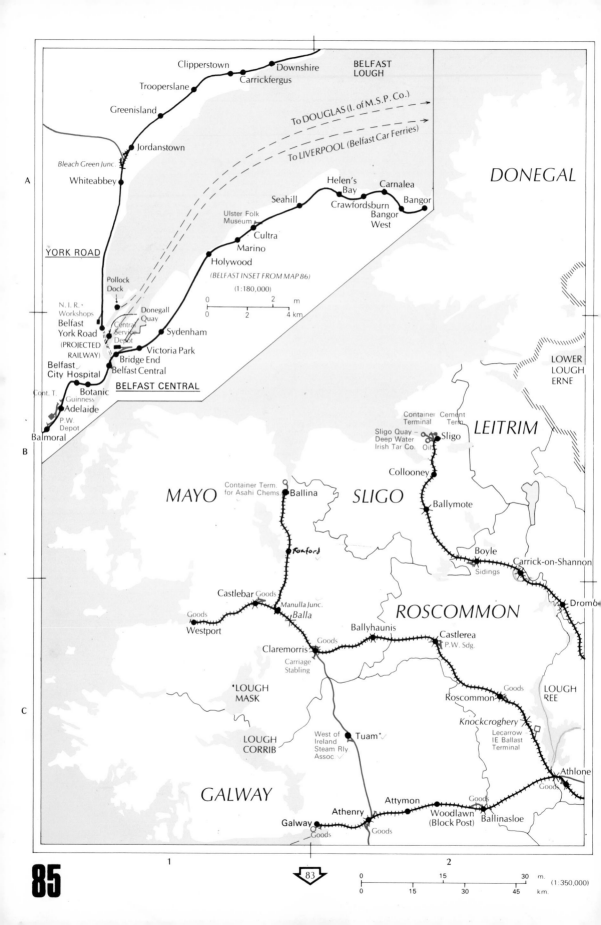

Clipperstown
Downshire
Carrickfergus
BELFAST
LOUGH
Trooperslane
Greenisland
Jordanstown
Bleach Green Junc.
Whiteabbey

To DOUGLAS (I. of M.S.P. Co.)
To LIVERPOOL (Belfast Car Ferries)

DONEGAL

Helen's
Bay
Carnalea
Seahill
Bangor
Crawfordsburn
Bangor
West
*Ulster Folk
Museum*
Cultra
Marino
Holywood

YORK ROAD

(BELFAST INSET FROM MAP 86)
(1:180,000)

0   2   m
0   2   4 km

Pollock
Dock
N. I. R.
Workshops
Donegall
Quay
Belfast
York Road
(PROJECTED
RAILWAY)
Central
Service
Depot
Sydenham
Victoria Park
Bridge End
Belfast Central
Belfast
City Hospital
Cont. T.
Guinness
Botanic
Adelaide
P.W.
Depot
Balmoral

BELFAST CENTRAL

LOWER
LOUGH
ERNE

Container
Terminal
Cement
Term.
Sligo Quay –
Deep Water
Irish Tar Co.
Oil
Sligo

LEITRIM

MAYO
Container Term.
for Asahi Chems.
Ballina

SLIGO
Colloney
Ballymote

Boyle
Sidings
Carrick-on-Shannon

Foxford

Castlebar
Goods
Manulla Junc.
Balla

ROSCOMMON

Dromo

Goods
Westport
Claremorris
Ballyhaunis
Castlerea
P.W. Sdg.
Carriage
Stabling

*LOUGH
MASK*

Goods
Roscommon

LOUGH
REE

Goods

Knockcroghery
Lecarrow
IE Ballast
Terminal

C

LOUGH
CORRIB

West of
Ireland
Steam Rly
Assoc.
Tuam

Athlone
Goods
Goods

GALWAY

Attymon
Goods
Athenry
Woodlawn
(Block Post)
Ballinasloe
Galway
Goods
Goods

1

83

2

0   15   30 m.
(1:350,000)
0   15   30   45 km.

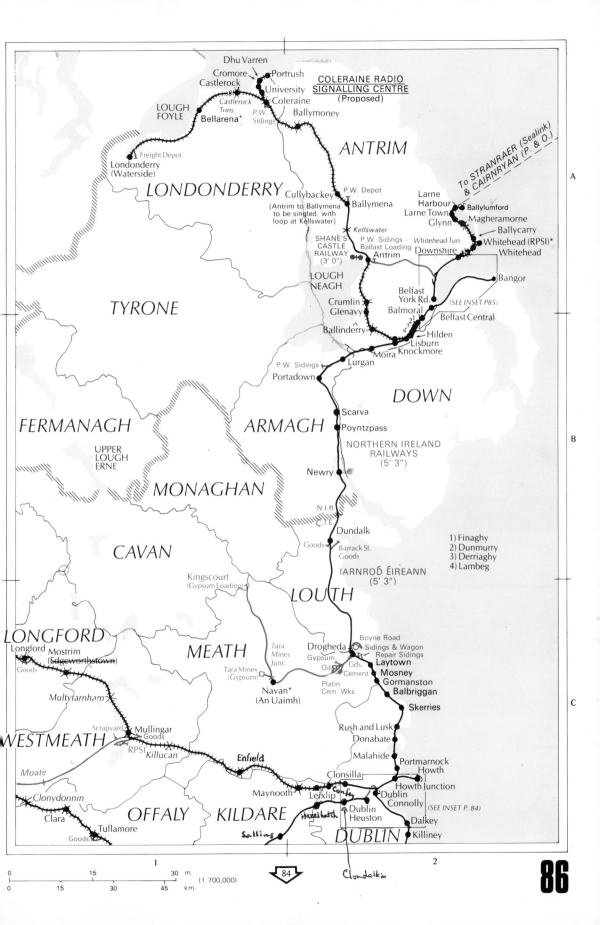

Dhu Varren
Cromore   Portrush
Castlerock
LOUGH   University
FOYLE   Castlerock   Coleraine
            Tuns.   Ballymoney
Bellarena*   P.W.
            Sidings

COLERAINE RADIO
SIGNALLING CENTRE
(Proposed)

ANTRIM

To STRANRAER (Sealink)
& CAIRNRYAN (P. & O.)

A

Freight Depot
Londonderry
(Waterside)

LONDONDERRY

Cullybackey   P.W. Depot
(Antrim to Ballymena   Ballymena
to be singled, with
loop at Kellswater)

Larne
Harbour   Ballylumford
Larne Town
Glynn   Magheramorne
            Ballycarry

TYRONE

Kellswater
SHANE'S   P.W. Sidings – Whitehead Tun.
CASTLE   Ballast Loading   Downshire
RAILWAY   Antrim
(3' 0")

Whitehead (RPSI)*
Whitehead

Bangor

LOUGH
NEAGH

Crumlin
Glenavy

Belfast
York Rd.
Balmoral   (SEE INSET P85)
21   Belfast Central

Ballinderry
            Hilden
            Lisburn
Moira   Knockmore
Lurgan

DOWN

FERMANAGH

UPPER
LOUGH
ERNE

P.W. Sidings
Portadown

ARMAGH

Scarva
Poyntzpass

NORTHERN IRELAND
RAILWAYS
(5' 3")

B

MONAGHAN

Newry

N.I.R.
C.I.E.

1) Finaghy
2) Dunmurry
3) Derriaghy
4) Lambeg

CAVAN

Goods
            Dundalk
            Barrack St.
            Goods

IARNRÓD ÉIREANN
(5' 3")

Kingscourt
(Gypsum Loading)

LOUTH

LONGFORD
Longford   Mostrim
Goods   (Edgeworthstown)

MEATH

Tara
Mines
Junc.

Tara Mines
(Gypsum)

Navan*
(An Uaimh)

Drogheda
Gypsum
Oil

Boyne Road
Sidings & Wagon
Repair Sidings

Gds.
Cement
Platin
Cem. Wks.

Laytown
Mosney
Gormanston
Balbriggan

Skerries

C

Multyfarnham

Mullingar
Scrapyard   Goods
RPSI   Killucan

WESTMEATH

Moate

Enfield

Maynooth

Clonsilla
Leixlip

Rush and Lusk
Donabate
Malahide
Portmarnock
Howth
Howth Junction
(SEE INSET P. 84)

Clonydonnin
Clara
Tullamore
Goods

OFFALY   KILDARE

Hazelhatch
Sallins

Dublin
Connolly

Dublin
Heuston

Clondalkin

DUBLIN

Dalkey
Killiney

0   15   30 m.
0   15   30   45 km.
(1 : 700,000)

1   84   2

86

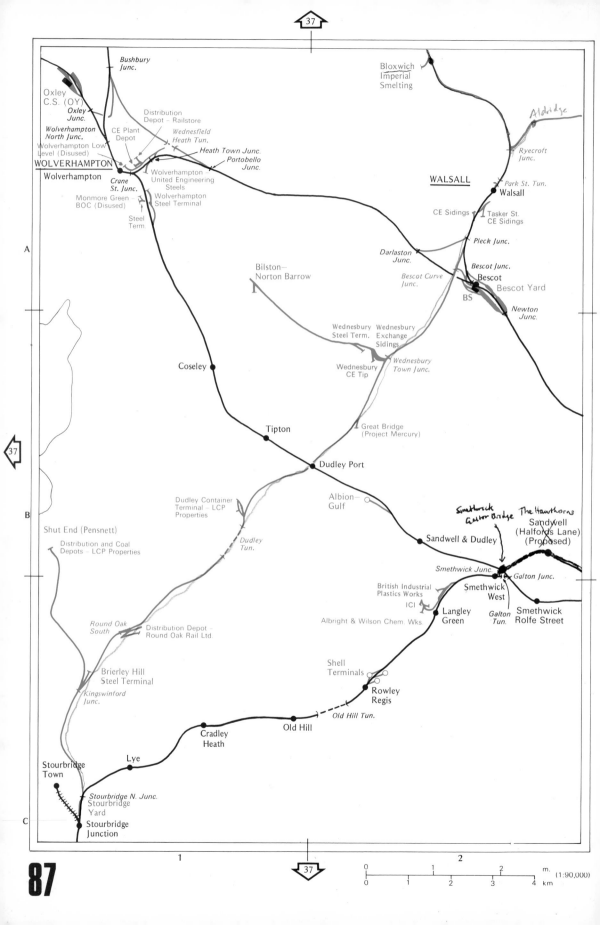

Bushbury Junc.

Bloxwich
Imperial
Smelting

Aldridge

Oxley
C.S. (OY)
*Oxley
Junc.*

*Wolverhampton
North Junc.*

Distribution
Depot – Railstore

*Wednesfield
Heath Tun.*

*Ryecroft
Junc.*

Wolverhampton Low
Level (Disused)

CE Plant
Depot

Heath Town Junc.

Portobello
Junc.

WALSALL

Park St. Tun.

Walsall

WOLVERHAMPTON

Wolverhampton

*Crane
St. Junc.*

Wolverhampton
United Engineering
Steels

CE Sidings

Tasker St.
CE Sidings

Monmore Green –
BOC (Disused)

Wolverhampton
Steel Terminal

Pleck Junc.

Steel
Term.

*Darlaston
Junc.*

Bescot Junc.

A

Bilston–
Norton Barrow

*Bescot Curve
Junc.*

Bescot

Bescot Yard

BS

*Newton
Junc.*

Wednesbury
Steel Term.

Wednesbury
Exchange
Sidings

Coseley

Wednesbury
CE Tip

*Wednesbury
Town Junc.*

Tipton

Great Bridge
(Project Mercury)

Dudley Port

Albion–
Gulf

Dudley Container
Terminal – LCP
Properties

*Smethwick
Galton Bridge* *The Hawthorns*

Sandwell
(Halfords Lane)
(Proposed)

B

Shut End (Pensnett)

*Dudley
Tun.*

Sandwell & Dudley

Distribution and Coal
Depots – LCP Properties

Smethwick Junc.

Galton Junc.

British Industrial
Plastics Works

Smethwick West

*Round Oak
South*

Distribution Depot –
Round Oak Rail Ltd.

ICI

Langley
Green

*Galton
Tun.*

Smethwick
Rolfe Street

Albright & Wilson Chem. Wks.

Brierley Hill
Steel Terminal

*Kingswinford
Junc.*

Shell
Terminals

Rowley
Regis

Old Hill Tun.

Cradley
Heath

Old Hill

Lye

Stourbridge
Town

Stourbridge N. Junc.

Stourbridge
Yard

C

Stourbridge
Junction

1

0   1   2   m. (1:90,000)
0   1   2   3   4   km

2

STAFFORDSHIRE

WARWICKS.

WEST
MIDLANDS

Blake
Street

Butlers
Lane

Four
Oaks   C.S.

Sutton Park
P.O.
Sutton Coldfield   Sutton
                         Coldfield
                         Tun.

A

Wylde
Green

Chester
Road

Erdington

Hamstead   Water
                  Orton
                  West
Perry Barr   Park   Junc.
North Junc.   Lane Junc.
Perry Barr
South Junc.   Imperial   Castle
Perry Barr   Metal Wks.   Bromwich Junc.
Jewellery Quarter   West Junc.   Gravelly Hill   Castle Bromwich   B
Handsworth   Perry Barr   – MEB
Boulton Rd.
(Proposed)   Witton   BSC   Castle Bromwich
Hamstead   Bromford   Castle Cem. Term.
Handsworth &   Tun.   Stone
Smethwick   Terminal   Washwood   Bromford
Blue Circle   Aston   Heath Yard   Bridge – Esso
Cem. Term.
Coopers   RMC Stone Terminal
Scrapyd.   Soho   Metro–Cammell
Soho   E. Junc.   C & W   Carriage Works
N. Junc.   Soho   Shops
Soho   S. Junc.   SALTLEY   Stechford
SI   (Projected   Duddeston   Lawley St. FLT
          Extension)   Sidings   Landor St. Junc.
          Snow   Castle Cem.   SY Adderley Park   Lea Hall
          Hill   Term.
Birmingham   Tun.   Curzon St
Snow Hill   Parcels
Birmingham   Proof   Grand   St Andrews Junc.
New St. North Tun.   New St.   House   Junc.
Holliday St. Tun.   Junc.
Canal Tun.   New   Bordesley Junc.
NEW ST.   Granville St. Tun.   St.   Bordesley Car
Bath Row Tun.   Sth.   Terminal – MAT
Five Ways   Tun.   Bordesley   Small Heath
          Suffolk   Birmingham   Small Heath South Junc.
          St. Tun.   Moor St.   Small Heath   DMU & C.S.
          Coal Depot -   Car Term. – Tolemans
          LCP Fuels   TS   Tyseley
Church   Norton Persto   Tyseley South Junc.
Road   Scrapyard   Standard Gauge   Allen
Tun.   Steam Trust   Rowland   Acocks Green
University   Works   C
Moseley Tun.

1   2

37

0   1   2   m. (1:90,000)
0 1 2 3 4 km

88

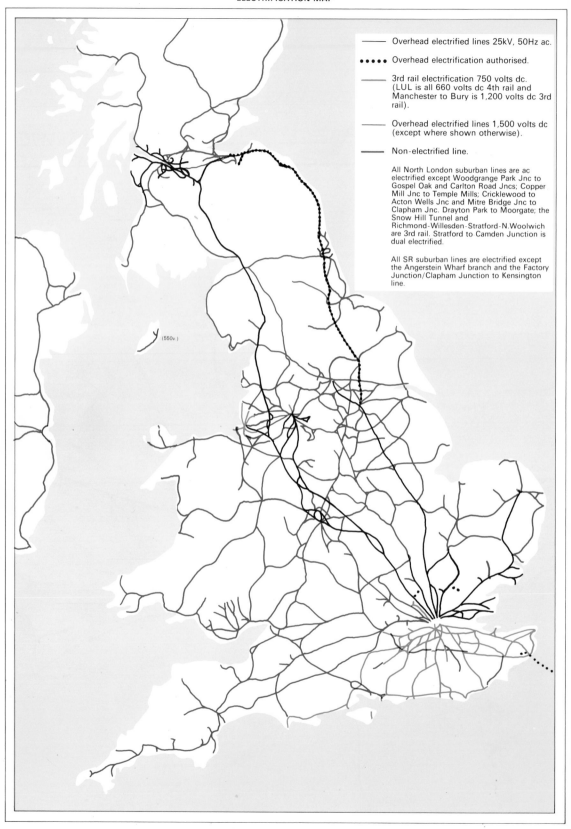

Overhead electrified lines 25kV, 50Hz ac.

Overhead electrification authorised.

3rd rail electrification 750 volts dc.
(LUL is all 660 volts dc 4th rail and
Manchester to Bury is 1,200 volts dc 3rd
rail).

Overhead electrified lines 1,500 volts dc
(except where shown otherwise).

Non-electrified line.

All North London suburban lines are ac
electrified except Woodgrange Park Jnc to
Gospel Oak and Carlton Road Jncs; Copper
Mill Jnc to Temple Mills; Cricklewood to
Acton Wells Jnc and Mitre Bridge Jnc to
Clapham Jnc. Drayton Park to Moorgate; the
Snow Hill Tunnel and
Richmond-Willesden-Stratford-N.Woolwich
are 3rd rail. Stratford to Camden Junction is
dual electrified.

All SR suburban lines are electrified except
the Angerstein Wharf branch and the Factory
Junction/Clapham Junction to Kensington
line.

(550v.)

GLOSSARY OF ABBREVIATIONS

ABM	Associated British Maltsters		L.L.	Low Level
ABP	Associated British Ports		LM	London Midland Region
AR	Anglia Region		LUL	London Underground Limited
ARC	Amey Roadstone Company		MDHC	Mersey Docks & Harbour Company
ASW	Allied Steel & Wire		M&EE	Mechanical and Electrical Engineer
B & I	British & Irish Line		MIFT	Manchester International Freight Terminal
BC	British Coal		MOD	Ministry of Defence
BICC	British Insulated Callenders Cables		MSC	Manchester Ship Canal
BIS	British Industrial Sand		NCL	National Carriers Limited
BOC	British Oxygen Company		NFD	National Fuel Distributors
BP	British Petroleum		NIR	Northern Ireland Railways
BR	British Rail		NSF	National Smokeless Fuels
BSC	British Steel Corporation		OLE	Overhead Line Equipment
BWB	British Waterways Board		PO	Post Office
C. & W.	Carriage and Wagon		P.S.	Power Station
Cal-Mac	Caledonian MacBrayne		PTE	Passenger Transport Executive
C.C.	County Council		P.W.	Permanent Way
CE	Civil Engineer		RHM	Rank Hovis McDougall
CEGB	Central Electricity Generating Board		RMC	Ready Mix Concrete (Marcon)
C.S.	Carriage Sidings		RPSI	Railway Preservation Society of Ireland
DCL	Distillers Company Limited		S. & T.	Signal & Telegraph
Dist.	Distribution		SAI	Scottish Agricultural Industries
D.P.	Disposal Point		SC	Scottish Region
ECC	English China Clays		SGD	Scottish Grain Distillers
EMU	Electric Multiple Unit		SMD	Scottish Malt Distillers
ER	Eastern Region		SO	Southern Region
FLT	Freightliner Terminal		Term.	Terminal
GEC	General Electric Company		UES	United Engineering Steels
H.L.	High Level		UKAEA	United Kingdom Atomic Energy Authority
ICI	Imperial Chemical Industries		UKF	United Kingdom Fertilisers
IE	Iarnród Éireann (Irish Rail)		WR	Western Region
LIFT	London International Freight Terminal			

INDEX

All passenger stations are included in this index. Freight terminals, junction names, tunnels and other significant locations are indexed where their names or maps references differ from an adjoining passenger station.

Broxbridge 8f *B1*

96

98

101

107

109

110

INDEX TO BRITISH RAIL
LOCOMOTIVE STABLING POINTS
& CARRIAGE DEPOTS